IRC & Online Chat

David Powers

Abacus

Copyright © 1997   Abacus
5370 52nd Street SE
Grand Rapids, MI 49512
www.abacuspub.com

This book is copyrighted. No part of this book may be reproduced, stored in a retrieval system, or transmitted in any form or by any means, electronic, mechanical, photocopying, recording or otherwise without the prior written permission of Abacus Software.

Every effort has been made to ensure complete and accurate information concerning the material presented in this book. However, Abacus Software can neither guarantee nor be held legally responsible for any mistakes in printing or faulty instructions contained in this book. The authors always appreciate receiving notice of any errors or misprints.

This book contains trade names and trademarks of several companies. Any mention of these names or trademarks in this book are not intended to either convey endorsement or other associations with this book.

Printed in the U.S.A.

ISBN 1-55755-333-5

10 9 8 7 6 5 4 3 2 1

IRC & Online Chat Contents

1. **Installing The Companion CD-ROM 1**
   Companion CD-ROM Contents 4

2. **Welcome To A New World 7**
   Some Quick Terminology 13
       Processor (CPU) 14
       Peripherals 14
       Modem 14
       Communication protocol 15
       GUI 15
       Video card 16
       RAM and ROM 16
       Operating system 17
       Hard drive 17

Contents

    Bits and bytes 18

    Buffer 18

    Window 19

Now That You've Gotten Online, What Do You Do?. 20

3. Popular Tools Internet Travelers Use .. 23

The Proprietary Services, Or How AOL Got So Popular 25

    Choosing a screen name 27

    Selecting a password 29

What Kind of Hieroglyph Was That? 30

    Abbreviations (or acronyms) 30

    Emoticons 31

    Instant Messages (IMs) 36

IRC 37

Web-Based Chat 49

Electronic Bulletin Boards 49

Virtual Places 52

Web Based Conference Chats 55

Enhanced CUSeeMe 56

VI

Contents

Videophone 60
Helpful Extras 63
Conclusion 64

4. Rules 65

The Written Rules 69
    Vulgarity 69
    Harassing people 70
    Sexually explicit 72
    Impersonation 72
    Scrolling 73
    Room disruption 73

The Unwritten Rules 74
Conclusion 75

5. How Not To Be An Online Embarrassment 77

Tips On Chatting Well 80
    How to be yourself 81
    Participate! 81

Contents

    Type the way you speak 84

    Be conversational 85

    Keep your own personality 87

Ways To Chat Poorly 88

    Personas outside of games 90

    Personal attacks 92

Conclusion 95

6. Dealing With Inappropriate Behavior . 97

Types Of Inappropriate Behavior 100

    Attention seekers 101

    Impolite or forward suggestors 109

    Unsolicited mail or messages 111

General Ways To Deal With Inappropriate Behavior 116

Conclusion 128

7. Who Are These People, Anyway? 129

Why Do People Chat? 132

    So what's the answer? Why do people chat? 132

    Meet people 136

Contents

    Games 138

    MUD (Multi-User Dungeon) 141

    Safe forums 155

    Resources 158

    Red light district 161

    Romance 164

    Support 165

Conclusion **166**

8. Safety On The Net 169

The Good Guys 172

    AOL's ordained structure of volunteers 172

    Guides 173

    Rangers 173

    People Connection Hosts 173

    Kids Only (KO) hosts 174

The Bad Guys 177

    Phishers 180

    Carding 186

    Warez 187

    Wormers 189

Contents

    Cyberpunks 190

    Phreakers 192

    Whacker 193

    Wannabe 195

    Online stalkers 195

Physical Security **198**

    Passwords and physical security measures 198

    Safety in meeting people from online 200

9. The End 203

Appendices

    Appendix A: Glossary 209

    Appendix B: Companion CD-ROM Contents 217

Index 235

What You'll Find On The Companion CD-ROM

Chapter 1

Companion CD-ROM Contents 4

Welcome to the IRC & Online Chat companion CD-ROM. We've included the best chat software for you to evaluate. The MENU program is the main screen to access the programs and files on the companion CD-ROM. Insert the companion CD-ROM in your drive.

Windows 3.x

To run the CD-ROM in Windows 3.x, select **Run...** from the **File** pull-down menu located at the top left corner of your screen (this is the Windows program Manager Screen). Type the following (where "d" is the device letter assigned to your CD-ROM drive):

```
d:\Menu.exe
```

and click the [OK] button. Click the [OK] button again and the Menu program will be loaded.

Installing The Companion CD-ROM

Chapter I

Windows 95

To run the CD-ROM in Windows 95, click the [Start] button, select **Run...** and type the following:

    d:\Menu.exe

Click the [OK] button. This will load the CD's Menu program.

The Main Menu

Select an item in the Main Menu by double-clicking on it.

Companion CD-ROM Contents

The following table lists and explains the contents of the companion CD-ROM. See Appendix B for a complete description of the contents of the companion CD-ROM:.

Installing The Companion CD-ROM

Chapter 1

Directory	Contents
ABACUS	Contains the electronic version of the Abacus Book & Software Catalog.
ATCHAT10	AtChat from Abbott Systems, Inc.
AWB	ActiveWorlds from Worlds, Inc.
CU30	CU-SeeMe Version 3.0 from White Pine Software, Inc.
CUSESS	CU-SeeMe Accessories from White Pine Software, Inc.
FERRET	NetFerret and IRCFerret from FerretSoft LLC.
ICIE222	ichat 32-bit plug-in chat utility from ichat, Inc.
LOLCHAT	Chat software from LOL Software, Inc.
MASQ140	Masquerade from HiJiNX Interactive Enterprises, Inc.
MIRCSO2T	mIRC from Khaled Mardam-Bey and mIRC Co., LTD.
NETGAMMON	Play Backgammon from GOTO.
PAGER	ichat Inc.'s Internet Pager evaluation.
POW WOW	and Kids' Pow Wow, personal communication chat software from Tribal Voice, Inc.
WPB	White Pine Software, Inc.'s WhitePine Board evaluation.
ZMUD	Zugg's Multi-User Dungeon Internet Software.
	Additional files including AT&T's WorldNet and CompuServe's Sprynet internet services sign-up programs.

5

Welcome To A New World

2

Chapter 2

Some Quick Terminology 13
  Processor (CPU) 14
  Peripherals 14
  Modem 14
  Communication protocol 15
  GUI 15
  Video card 16
  RAM and ROM 16
  Operating system 17
  Hard drive 17
  Bits and bytes 18
  Buffer 18
  Window 19
Now That You've Gotten Online, What Do You Do? .. 20

Suppose one balmy July day in Chicago, you decide to go to Sydney, New South Wales, and spend a month. You pack up 6 light outfits, call your travel agent for a ticket, hop onto the plane and go.

The first thing you're going to notice when you get off that plane is that you're woefully under-dressed. July is mid-winter in Australia and all you have are your summer clothes. You'll probably also notice that although the natives are speaking English, it's laced with phrases and words you've never heard. All in all, you're probably not going to have an easy trip, nor the most pleasant one, as you acclimate on a minute-by-minute basis from your American lifestyle to Oz. No one would really make a trip with that little preparation, though, now would they?

Welcome To A New World

Chapter 2

Actually, I see them do it all the time. Not flying to Australia on a whim, no, but flying to a cross-cultural, multinational, two-dimensional land where the people speak mostly English, but a new dialect of it, rich with acronyms and pictographs. This land is commonly called *Cyberspace* and it's online as close as your monitor. Visitors to this country are suddenly faced with lines of text interspersed with "afk brb :)". "What kind of hieroglyphic is that?" these people wonder.

Joe is a new computer user. His brand-new Pentium-based PC with 64 Meg of RAM and a 200 Megahertz chip is top of the line. It comes complete with a 33,600 baud modem and bundled software allowing him access to a popular online service called America Online that he's seen advertised on television hundreds of times.

This software automatically detects modem and port, requires very little setup and is totally GUI (it uses a graphic interface), making it attractive, colorful and self-explanatory.

> *As soon as he opens the door, he's spun into a mad world of line after line of someone called "Online Host" announcing "You are in Lobby 957," "Member423 has left the room," "MemberHEG has entered the room,"*

A few minutes later Joe is online in the cyberworld. He's looking at a bewildering screen with a tool bar across the top and a multicolored, multi-option menu in the center. A friendly voice says "Welcome," startling him, then he's alone in the virtual train station. He hasn't brought any luggage with him, so he takes a breath, looks up and down the many doors of the station. He finally chooses one, opening it with a click of his mouse: "People Connection."

As soon as he opens the door, he's spun into a mad world of line after line of someone called "Online Host" announcing "You are in Lobby 957," "Member423 has left the room," "MemberHEG has entered the room," "Member957 has left the room," "Member874

Welcome To A New World

Chapter 2

has left the room." Then a line preceded by "SexHund65" appears: "PRESS 69 IF U'RE HORNY." This is followed by an amazingly intricate and anatomically correct picture.

Joe looks over the screen and finally locates a button called "List Chats." He clicks it and is presented with a dizzying array of chats, hundreds of them on just the one list, and he can see by clicking other categories that there are hundreds more. Being a sports fan, he locates a likely looking candidate, "Bulls Chat," and dives in.

Here again he sees Online Host with the constant drone of entering and exiting members. Here, though, people are talking. "BULLS RULE," notes one member. "THEY SUCK," another argues. "Could you people stop talking in all caps?" whines another.

Joe finally decides it's time to do something here. "HEY, ARE ANY OF YOU IN CHICAGO?" he types. To his dismay, he's completely ignored. Suddenly, he hears the friendly train man announce "You've got mail!" Joe clicks the inviting flag and finds a letter from SnErT7564 with a free upgrade to Word for Windows attached. He downloads the file according to the directions, logs off and restarts his computer.

> *The web and the Internet are full of people who, under the cloak of anonymity, find ways to act out all the impulses they have to restrain in everyday life.*

When he opens Word, however, he finds no change to it. Puzzled, he logs back to tell SnErT7564 the file seems to have not worked. When he tries to send mail to SnErT7564, he receives a message that this is no longer a member. Really confused now, Joe logs off and tries Word again. When he tries to log back on to AOL a few hours later, he is greeted by a log-off screen and the explanation that this account has been terminated for violations of the Terms of Service.

Welcome To A New World

Chapter 2

So what happened? Put simply, Joe ventured into a foreign country without a map. He had no clue how to get to areas with people who shared his interests, and ended up downloading a file called a "password sniffer" distributed by thieves who prey on new arrivals, stealing their accounts and using them to disrupt until they manage to get canceled. Is this unique to America Online? No, not at all!

The web and the Internet are full of people who, under the cloak of anonymity, find ways to act out all the impulses they have to restrain in everyday life. The Internet is like any large city, it has its good districts and its crime ridden ones, with people ranging from good hearted Samaritans to people who have nothing better to do than torment and hurt.

Just as you wouldn't go to Sydney without the slightest clue what do when you got there, you need to be prepared before you head out to participate in online chat in any of its wondrous forms.

A basic knowledge of your computer, several important terms, and the different methods of chat will help you tremendously to be successful.

How many forms are there? There's a few, to be sure! The ones you will most likely come into contact with are:

- Internet Relay Chat (IRC)
- E-mail
- Web-based chat
- Video conferencing
- Proprietary online services' chat rooms
- Instant messages

Welcome To A New World

Chapter 2

For ease of explanation, I'm going to stick to easy-to-access forms of each of these media. You access a chat through its "client." For IRC, we'll be using an easily acquired client called "MIRC," and I'll be telling you how to get it.

The example proprietary service is America Online, whose software is available for free in any computing magazine or by mail. That's also our model Email server. For web-based chat we're going to delve into CUSeeMe, which uses a video camera.

We'll also look at the text-based "Virtual Places," which is non-visual web chat. For video conferencing one on one, we'll use Connectix Videophone, a commercial product available at most software stores or bundled with the QuickCam.

While this group of products is by no means exhaustive of what's available, they represent for the most part the easiest to obtain and least expensive types of each of these chat media.

Some Quick Terminology

As you have undoubtedly already noticed, there are a lot of terms to learn before you ever log online! I'm going to take a quick break here to explain some of these.

Remember, the more you know about the equipment and technology you're using, the more successful you will be at using it. Indy 500 race car drivers and your 16-year old learning to drive for the first time are using the same skills, but the Indy racer knows a lot more about the car and how its design affects the overall performance, so he's able to accomplish more with the same skills.

Welcome To A New World

Chapter 2

Processor (CPU)

Briefly, your computer's brain is the *processor*, called the "CPU" (Central Processing Unit). Its speed is measured in megahertz and refers to how many cycles of information it can process in a second. The higher this number, the faster it is.

Peripherals

The CPU communicates with the peripherals to accomplish tasks. A *peripheral* is anything extra connected to your computer that's not required for it to function as a computer. This includes sound cards, video cards, modems, mice, joysticks, video cameras, speakers, zip drives, tape drives and the neighbor's refrigerator (if you have the proper cabling).

Modem

A *modem* is a peripheral designed to translate audio signals, which are analog, into digital signals the processor is able to decode. The word itself is a shortening of its function: **mo**dulate/**dem**odulate.

The modem receives an analog instruction set for the processor via the telephone lines. It translates that signal into digital and sends it to the processor. The processor completes the instruction set and creates one of its own. The modem then retranslates the signal received from the processor back into analog and sends it through an analog phone line to the computer with which it is communicating.

The data's transmission speed is determined primarily by the modem's speed (28.8 or 33.6 kilobits per second are the current standards) and the quality of your telephone lines.

Welcome To A New World

Chapter 2

Communication protocol

When the modem connects you'll hear a handshake. This series of whines and clicks is how one computer establishes protocol with the other computer, protocol being the common language they will use. *Communication protocol* is in two layers:

- IP
- TCP

IP is responsible for moving packets of data from node to node. IP forwards each packet based on a four byte destination address (the IP number). The Internet authorities assign ranges of numbers to different organizations. The organizations assign groups of their numbers to departments. IP operates on gateway machines that move data from department to organization to region and then around the world.

Because data can be lost during transmission, TCP is responsible for verifying the correct delivery of data from client to server. TCP detects errors or lost data and triggers retransmission until the data is correctly and completely received.

GUI

GUI (pronounced "gooey") is short for "Graphic User Interface." This means that it has pictures, not just pure text. Mac operating systems are generally GUI, as are the proprietary services we'll be looking at for Windows 95. Windows 95 itself is GUI, but you can go to the text-based DOS to see the difference.

All these graphics require that you have enough RAM (Random Access Memory) and a video card to see them.

Welcome To A New World

Chapter 2

Video card

The *video card* is built into your computer, and it translates the signal to your monitor. Having a Super VGA (SVGA) video card and monitor will make these graphics even better. A video accelerator card can also help, and is easily obtained at any computer hardware store. But it doesn't matter what kind of video card and accelerators you have installed if your monitor is only capable of supporting VGA graphics.

Your computer's hardware is only as upgraded as its lowest component, so make sure the video card and the monitor are matched in this regard, or you've wasted money on one or the other, as you won't be able to see the fancy graphics for which you paid.

RAM and ROM

RAM is one of the two types of memory in your computer. Your computer also has an integrated memory circuit called a *ROM chip*. This chip has the basic setup instructions for your computer. It tells your computer who it is and how it's configured so it boots the same way for you each time. This also tells your computer to look for operating systems, the autoexec.bat file and the config.sys to start your computer's programs.

RAM is the memory you use while working with your computer. It contains your buffers (areas where data is stored while it's in use) and is wiped clean when you shut down. It's a dynamic type of memory, which means its contents are constantly changing as you use the machine. The more RAM you have, the smoother your computer will run and the more programs you will be able to run simultaneously.

Welcome To A New World

Chapter 2

In addition, more RAM allows you to run larger programs. Programs' documentation will tell you how much RAM you need to run them minimally, but don't expect them to run optimally at that level. You can never have too much RAM.

Operating system

The *operating system* is what tells your computer how to run once it's booted. This set of instructions controls how programs interact with the hardware and other software within your system. DOS, Macintosh, UNIX, Windows NT and Windows 95 are among the most popular operating systems.

Windows 3.x is a shell for DOS, providing a graphic interface. The Mac O/S is a true operating system, while SoftWindows is a shell that allows you to run some Windows programs on a Macintosh. You'll find you have better luck running programs on real operating systems, as opposed to shells.

The operating system requires some of your RAM to run, so always subtract that amount from the total physical RAM you have installed to find the amount of available RAM. A machine with 8 Megabytes of RAM running Windows 95 only has about 1 Megabyte of RAM left for running programs.

Hard drive

A *hard drive* is not memory. The terms can be kind of confusing, since memory in a human mind is where we store information we need to retrieve. Looking closer at that definition though, we can see what a hard drive actually is: storage. This is where you're going to put your programs, documents, etc. until you need them. This is where you save to, and this is from where you pull up items and launch programs. Think of this as your long-term memory, whereas

Welcome To A New World

Chapter 2

your RAM is your short term, which is erased when new data enters it, and which is always changing. Your hard drive only changes when you order it to do so, by removing data or saving a new file.

Bits and bytes

The operating system we're working with is Windows 95, a 32-bit operating system. A *bit* is 8 bytes, and a *byte* is one character, either a zero or a one. Every letter you see on this page was constructed using these zeros and ones. There are 16-bit operating systems, which use packets of information sent 16 at a time, and there are 32-bit operating systems, using packets of information sent 32 at a time, or 32 characters long.

As you can imagine, 32-bit operating systems are faster than 16-bit operating systems. In addition, using the correct software for each of these systems makes that software run better. You can usually run a Windows 3.1x program on Windows 95, but Windows 3.1x is 16 bit. By running the same program with a Windows 95 version, using a 32-bit program with a 32-bit operating system, you can take advantage of the functions and speed available in Windows 95.

Buffer

A *buffer* is where information is stored within RAM. There are several different kinds of buffers, but the ones we're concerned with are text or chat buffers. This is where a single sentence or two can be stored to be sent to screen.

By having buffer, a user can compose a sentence, proofread it, then send it out in a modified form. If you didn't have a buffer, you would only be able to type real time, which would not be nearly so tidy! Without buffers, each character you typed would go immediately to screen, with all your typographical errors.

Welcome To A New World

Chapter 2

You can usually find the chat buffer in an online chat application at the bottom of the channel or room you're in. Typically, the conversation will flow in a double-paned window, the top of which is the channel and the bottom of which is the chat buffer. In the case of MUDs and BBSes, which we'll go over later, the chat buffer will be at the bottom of the Telnet application's window, while all activity will occur within the window.

Window

A window is the area onscreen where a program performs some or all of its functions. You can have several windows open at any one time, usually within any application.

For instance, if you have Word open, its main area will be a window. Within Word, you may have three documents open, and each of these is also a window. You may have AOL open, which shows a main window, and within it have a room window, three IM windows and a forum's main screen window, while a browser window you have minimized is down in the lower right corner of your screen. Each window needs RAM to display it, so remember to keep the number of windows you have open to a minimum to avoid running out of memory.

I know this all seems like so much technobabble right now, but when we get to the sections on video conferencing, you will find it invaluable. By understanding how IP addressing works, for instance, you can readily understand why some versions of America Online won't work with it.

Welcome To A New World

Chapter 2

Now That You've Gotten Online, What Do You Do?

There are a few answers to this question, which is best answered with another question: what do you want to do? There are various ways of conducting online chat, depending on what you're looking for.

The proprietary services offer forums as well as specialized chat rooms for topic-themed chats. IRC has literally thousands of channels per server, for any type of conversation you'd ever want to hold on any number of topics.

Web-based chat and video conferencing offer the same variety of chat, only they allow visual and aural content and often involve extra peripherals such as cameras, microphones and speakers, and also permit the creation of avatars (a picture used to represent a person).

So the first thing you have to decide is what you're looking for. Proprietary services offer the easiest access and are the simplest way to get started in online chat so we'll be looking at them first. Next easiest is IRC, which requires some knowledge of networking and winsock manipulation to get started.

The video-based chats use more advanced technology, requiring some grasp of bandwidth and frame rate capability as well as modem compression.

> *The easiest way to use this book will be to go to your computer, boot it up, install each piece as we go, and don't be afraid to mark in the book or bend the covers.*

Welcome To A New World

Chapter 2

While I will be looking at these things in brief, if you're not comfortable "tweaking" your system and software, this may not be the choice for you.

The easiest way to use this book will be to go to your computer, boot it up, install each piece as we go, and don't be afraid to mark in the book or bend the covers. Look at it as your tour guide, and treat it accordingly. Ready? Let's go!

Popular Tools Internet Travelers Use

3

Chapter 3

The Proprietary Services, Or How AOL Got So Popular	**25**
Choosing a screen name	27
Selecting a password	29
What Kind of Hieroglyph Was That?	**30**
Abbreviations (or acronyms)	30
Emoticons	31
Instant Messages (IMs)	36
IRC	**37**
Web-Based Chat	**49**
Electronic Bulletin Boards	**49**
Virtual Places	**52**
Web Based Conference Chats	**55**
Enhanced CUSeeMe	**56**
Videophone	**60**
Helpful Extras	**63**
Conclusion	**64**

The Proprietary Services, Or How AOL Got So Popular

I'm going to start at the very beginning, so if you already have America Online installed on your computer, pass this section over. To get an AOL diskette or CD, you can telephone the company's customer service at 800-827-6364. This is a free software diskette. You can also obtain a disk bundled in some computer magazines. AOL's client software is free, but there is a membership fee. This is true of most Internet service providers that are not educational institutions.

AOL's client will install itself using the modem settings you have set in Windows 95 via a driver called a "TAPI" (Telephony Application Programming Interface).

Popular Tools Internet Travelers Use

Chapter 3

Therefore, you want to be sure this is set up correctly. By clicking Start/Settings/Control Panels you can access the modem control panel. The first window you will see has a tab on top labeled "General." By clicking "Properties" you can verify your modem's port (usually Com 1, but not always) and speed. If you have a 28.8 or faster modem, set the speed to 57600, otherwise use the actual speed of your modem. When your settings are correct click [OK].

Click the control panel called "Add/Remove Programs" and insert the AOL diskette or CD-ROM. Click [Install...] on the Add/Remove Programs Properties dialog box.

Add/Remove Programs

Then click the [Next >] button.

Popular Tools Internet Travelers Use

Chapter 3

Windows 95 will search the floppy drive for a setup executable file, then present you with a window listing what it found. If the file listed is not correct, click [Browse...] and locate the AOL setup file, called "setup.exe."

Otherwise, all you need to do here is click [Finish] and let it install. Installing in this manner creates a log of the installation for Windows 95 to refer to if you choose to remove it later.

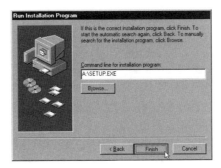

AOL's setup will now connect you to a bulletin board system listing AOL access numbers where you may choose a node (a point of entry to AOL's system). Typing your area code into the provided dialog box will bring you to a screen of area nodes. Choose numbers that are not long distance for you since your membership does not cover your phone charges! AOL will then log you off the BBS and dial the number you selected as your access number.

Choosing a screen name

At this point you will be prompted to choose a screen name. Here's where a lot of new folks make their first mistake, so we'll delve a bit into net manners. We'll explain net etiquette (or *netiquette*) more fully a little later.

27

Popular Tools Internet Travelers Use

Chapter 3

Typing in all uppercase letters is considered yelling

Typing with the shift lock depressed (in all uppercase letters) is considered yelling in online communities. Your screen name will appear before every line of chat you send in a "room," and will be your Email address for AOL, as well as serving other purposes. Typing your screen name in all uppercase letters, therefore, is not something you want to do unless your intent is to scream your name at the top of your lungs with every line of text you send. In addition, this name is how people you meet will know you.

Your screen name is the impression you make

It might seem funny at the time to designate yourself by a private bodily measurement. However, think of how amusing it will be when you need to tell someone who matters to you that your Email address is thik9inch@aol.com. Remember when choosing your screen name that people online will not be able to see you, so this name is the impression you make, and that you may have this name for a long time. You can control this impression somewhat with the name you choose.

Avoid gender specific names

Unfortunately, some people lose online most traces of civility when they're protected by anonymity, so you might want to avoid gender specific names to prevent unwanted harassment by these people. Good choices for names might include hobbies, occupation (my own screen name on AOL reflects my occupation), pet names or fantasy or fictional characters you admire.

Popular Tools Internet Travelers Use

Chapter 3

Other hints

Don't choose names of living people you admire! Impersonation is a serious issue. It can even result in the loss of your AOL account. Remember also that a screen name that's too generic can make you appear to be bland yourself, so exercise some creativity and have fun with it!

The first letter of your new name will be capitalized automatically. Carefully check the spelling before accepting this name! Once entered, your master account name (the one you create first) can't be changed. You will have the opportunity to create up to four more names on this same account at no extra charge, and these can be changed at will.

Choosing a screenname		
Poor	Reason	Better
Trge557	Hard to remember	Tigr557
JOHNNYC	All caps	JohnNYC
Sex4Uhere	Vulgar	-

Selecting a password

Now that you've chosen your screen name, you need to select a password. Look at this password as the key to your account and make sure it's secure!

Don't use a pet's name, your screen name, your birthday, your children's names or any word that can be found in a standard dictionary. Choosing a word then changing one or two characters to digits is the best way to create a secure password.

For instance, you can take the word "menopaws" (which has 8 letters, and is somewhat unusual, making it fairly secure) and change it to "men0paws," making it even tougher to guess. Never tell

Popular Tools Internet Travelers Use

Chapter 3

ANYONE your password. There's no legitimate reason for anyone to need it, and it grants full access to your account. (Even AOL employees won't ever ask for it.)

What Kind of Hieroglyph Was That?

Once you get into the chat areas on AOL, mIRC or either of the video conferencing clients, you will find that chat uses a new language dialect of it's own. Since most online chat is conducted via a keyboard, a system of "shorthands" has developed allowing people to use fewer keystrokes. As with any language, these are constantly changing, and are often personalized as well. Therefore, use this section as a guide only.

Basically, shorthands fall into two categories:

1. Abbreviations
2. Emoticons

Abbreviations (or acronyms)

Abbreviations (or acronyms) place the first letters of the words in a phrase side-by-side. When you construct these, they should be terms that are used everyday, fairly regularly, and by many people. You'll get a feel for them quickly. Some people also will put several on a line to spell out an entire thought in a few keystrokes.

Below are some of the most common:

Popular Tools Internet Travelers Use

Chapter 3

Shortcut	Phrase	Shortcut	Phrase
bbiaf	be back in a few	lol	laughing out loud
afk	away from keyboard	rofl	rolling on floor laughing
bak	back at keys	bbiab	be back in a bit
brb	be right back	fas	for a second
lmao	laughing my *butt* off	btw	by the way
ttfn	ta-ta for now!	imho	in my humble opinion
wb	welcome back	wtg	way to go!
gmta	great minds think alike	imo	in my opinion

Emoticons

Because it is difficult (when not impossible) to convey tone and body language through text, many chatters use *emoticons*, a system of symbols that convey emotions or intent. By grouping several keystrokes to create a portrait of the speaker, one can differentiate between humorous sarcasm and serious intent. ":)" is one of the most basic. If you read it as "colon, end parenthesis," try turning the page sideways so the colon is above the parenthesis. Can you see the smiley face?

> *One of the most basic emoticons is ":)". If necessary, turn the page sideways so the colon is above the parenthesis. Can you see the smiley face?*

There are many variations of this basic emoticon, including ":(" for sadness and ";-)" as a winking smiley face (with a nose) and ":D" for a big grin. As you explore online you'll see many more of these.

Equipped with access and basic netiquette, you're now ready to get on the system! Log on, then click the icon of the two faces you will find near the top of your screen. Below is typical of what you'll see when you do so.

31

Popular Tools Internet Travelers Use

Chapter 3

(Don't panic, the names have been intentionally blurred in this and other illustrations in this chapter.)

The accompanying chat goes something like this (the names have been changed):

OnlineHost:	*** You are in "Town Square - Lobby 182". ***
OnlineHost:	
SNLPepers:	i didnt say antything
PAPER47:	CYA
OnlineHost:	MDAM100 has left the room.
OnlineHost:	SIMPLFLIE has entered the room.
SNLPepers:	i thought u did
SNLPepers:	no it wasn't me
OnlineHost:	Duckyboy9 has left the room.
OnlineHost:	AUSSIE56 has entered the room.
SNLPepers:	what shut up
SNLPepers:	no u shut up
RMacart04:	p.s. JHutchins is sick look out 4 him
OnlineHost:	Talk2me41 has left the room.

Popular Tools Internet Travelers Use

Chapter 3

OnlineHost:	Shamac3 has entered the room.
OnlineHost:	DOSEAGA4U has left the room.
OnlineHost:	Luvzi4 has entered the room.
RMacart04:	bye
AUSSIE56:	are there any girls in here that want to chat??
SNLPepers:	what u say to me !!??!?
SNLPepers:	i said shut up

There are several things to look at here. Note that the text is preceded by a screen name and a colon. You don't have to type that in when you chat, it's there automatically. Also, note there is something called "Online Host." This is not a person, but rather a piece of the AOL software. If it becomes distracting, you can turn it off by clicking "Members" at the top, then choosing "Preferences." Selecting "Chat Room" from this area will allow you to access selections marked "Notify me when members arrive" and "Notify me when members leave."

Take the "X"s out of the boxes to turn off the Online Host. Some people attempt to chat with Online Host. That's along the same lines as chatting with your doorbell. The example is typical lobby chat, which is where you are when you first sign onto AOL.

The main thing I want to point out is that there's not much chat here. It's possible to strike up a conversation, and some lobbies become meeting places of small groups of regulars, which can be a lot of fun. However, that takes a bit of skill in chatting.

The easiest way to find an appropriate area for you to chat is to click on the List Chats icon, then choose one of the themed chats you'll see listed. There are two categories:

Popular Tools Internet Travelers Use

Chapter 3

1. Member

2. Public

Both are public areas and are under the Terms of Service agreement you promised to abide by when you first logged onto AOL. However, Member rooms are chat areas created by members, while Public rooms are created by AOL.

To create a member room yourself, click on "List Chats" at the bottom of the chat screen. Choose "Member Rooms." From this screen, choose "Create Member Room." Type in the room name you want to create, then choose the [OK] button.

Now click on a themed chat room that looks promising. (Again and throughout, the names have been changed.)

OnlineHost:	
OnlineHost:	*** You are in "Slowhand". ***
OnlineHost:	
ClptonFrk:	had to change the CD
ClptonFrk:	Derek and the Dominos :)
Best818:	Layla!!!!!
ClptonFrk:	that's it!
Best818:	Got me on my knees, I'm beggin pretty please!
ClptonFrk:	song's about Patti Boyd Harrison
Best818:	Yeah, that was a weird situatioin wasn't it?

Popular Tools Internet Travelers Use

Chapter 3

ClptonFrk:	Slowhand's a wife stealer <g>
Best818:	And now he's alone isn't he?
ClptonFrk:	the name is from a goddess who started a war between two countries
ClptonFrk:	I don't remember the goddess's name, it's Hindu
Best818:	I'm not terribly well versed on Hindu, the only one I remember is Kali, goddess of
ClptonFrk:	the man who helped write this song is in prison for killing his mother with
Best818:	destruction and death! Nice chick!!
ClptonFrk:	a sledge hammer
ClptonFrk:	so it goes <g>
Best818:	Woah, I haden't heard that one.
ClptonFrk:	<—total Clapton junkie

This chat room has fewer members moving in and out of it. You see we entered during a conversation about Slowhand, Eric Clapton, after whom the room is named. These are two experienced chatters, which is evidenced in at least two ways:

* There are typographical errors, which happen frequently, yet the two participants have no trouble chatting. The errors don't mean anything to either one.

* Several shorthands (or symbols) are used that both understand. The next chapter talks about these more specifically, but the two in this clip are "<g>," which is a grin, and "<— " an arrow referring back to the speaker.

Popular Tools Internet Travelers Use

Chapter 3

Instant Messages (IMs)

Another way you can chat on America Online is via Instant Messages, called "IMs." These small windows look like this:

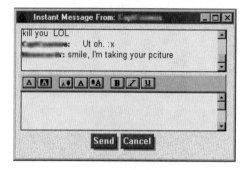

(Don't panic, the names have been intentionally blurred in this illustration.)

This private conversation window is a way to hold chats without anyone else being able to observe the conversation. In fact, you don't even have to be "in" a room or on a channel to have an instant message conversation, as long as you know the screen name of the person to whom you'd like to talk!

For over a year now I've held most of my online chats via Instant Message, finding them more manageable than chat rooms. Of course, before that can be done, you'll need to be fluent in chat rooms and have met a group of people with whom to regularly chat. Otherwise, you have no one to send an instant message to. I've actually had people ask me, "How do you know who to send an instant message to?" This question is akin to asking how do you know whose house to visit!

Popular Tools Internet Travelers Use

Chapter 3

IRC

IRC is like an AOL chat room in some important ways and unlike it in others. Internet Relay Chat, or IRC, is a way for many people all over the world to gather together in one area, called a "channel," in order to communicate. In this way, it's like an AOL chat room. Users of an IRC have the power to create themed rooms and to created personas in the form of screen names, also like AOL.

Unlike AOL, users who create rooms become the owners of those rooms. There is no public or private section of IRC; all rooms are created by users, some of which can then be designated as Private or Secret.

> *IRC is a chat area located on a server but it is not owned by a service—in other words, you don't pay to log on to an IRC server. To use an IRC server, you must have software allowing you to access an IRC and display it.*

IRC is a chat area located on a server but it is not owned by a service—in other words, you don't pay to log on to an IRC server. You pay your Internet service provider, which you use to log on to an IRC server. To use an IRC server, you have to have software that will allow you to access an IRC and display it.

From AOL, you can use Keyword http://www.mirc.co.uk/ to download mIRC, a client for entering IRC channels, on which AOL chat rooms are modeled. Make sure that you choose the 16-bit version!

The AOL we've set you up with is a 16-bit application, and you can't use a 32-bit application with it. Think of it like trying to drive a semi-tractor trailer down a one lane alley. On the Information Superhighway, you have 16-bit "lanes" and 32-bit "lanes," and while you can use a 16-bit application (truck) through a 32-bit client (lane), you can't go the other way around.

Popular Tools Internet Travelers Use

Chapter 3

As of this writing, the latest version of mIRC is version 5.0, which is the one we'll be using in this book. This is a free download of "shareware" software. Shareware gives you a chance to try it out and evaluate it before paying the small $15 price of the product. Always register shareware software! There are always clear instructions on how to do so, usually for a nominal fee, and it's how these developers get paid. First rule of netiquette: it's tacky to steal shareware software.

From the main page, choose DOWNLOAD at the bottom, then select a site close to you. This will bring up an FTP (File Transfer Protocol) dialog, requesting you to select where you would like the file placed. Choose either a folder you have created exclusively for mIRC or place it in the root directory. I always download large zipped files to my external 100 Meg removable drive, just to keep them handy and in one place. This file is approximately 804 kilobytes in size, taking about ten minutes to download using a 28.8 Kb modem.

Once you've downloaded the software, log off AOL and close down the program. Click on Start/Settings/Control Panels once again to choose "Add/Remove Programs." This time, you need to locate the file you have just downloaded. After you locate it, click install and allow Windows to install mIRC 5.0. It'll create a program group and put it in your Start menu so you can locate it easily once it's installed.

Please keep the defaults set for you when you install mIRC, which are to create icons and create backup files. If anything was to go wrong in the installation, you'll need those files. When mIRC has installed, it will invite you to read the read.me and faq files included. This is a good idea, as it will give you more in-depth information on how to use the client itself.

After installation, three windows will open on your desktop: the Add/Remove Programs window, mIRC program group and Control Panels. Close these windows after you have read through the help

Popular Tools Internet Travelers Use

Chapter 3

and read.me files in the mIRC program group. Now you're ready to launch mIRC. First, log on to AOL. Now, click the flat line in the upper right hand corner of the AOL screen, which will minimize it while leaving you logged on. At this point, click on Start/Programs. You'll see the mIRC 5.0 group on this list if you accepted the defaults at installation. Choose mIRC from here. The first screen is the registration screen which tells you how to register the software. Close this window by clicking on the "X" in the upper right hand corner.

mIRC set up screen

Now you have a set up screen. Use caution in filling out this screen, as this information is going to be accessible by anyone on the IRC server to which we will eventually connect. Refer to the figure above as we go through the steps to prepare mIRC for logging on for the first time.

Fill out your name or give a fictitious one in the first field. Again, please remember the second rule of netiquette: it's tacky to pretend to be someone you aren't. Fill out your Email address in the next

Popular Tools Internet Travelers Use

Chapter 3

field (again, this is accessible by anyone on the IRC server, so use your best judgment as to whether you want to enter your own or a fictitious name.

The next field you see is "nickname." This corresponds to your screen name on AOL, but it can be anything you want. Use the same thought processes to picking this name as you did your screen name on AOL. Also, if this name is in use on the server you're using, you'll need to use another one, so be sure to fill out the final field, "alternative." Leave "invisible mode" clicked off for now. This is for sysops and others who work with the IRC server administration.

Click on the tab marked "local info." This should be blank at this point. If it's not, delete anything you may see in there. This allows mIRC to locate your server, which is AOL right now. Make sure "local host" is checked and "normal" is marked for method. You want to have this set to local host so mIRC isn't looking for a remote user, which would be someone on your network accessing mIRC from their computer logged into your computer.

Click on the tab marked "options," and be sure only "pop-up dialog on start up" is checked and that the default port is set to 6667. Having anything beside "pop-up dialog on start up" checked would just create a bunch of windows for you to close. Port setting 6667 is a standard port setting, the lowest one of four. Setting it here gives you a standard default setting when you go to setup IRC logons later.

Click on the tab marked "Identd" and make sure "Enable" is not checked, which would force you to enter a password at every log-on, and that there is no information entered save the word "UNIX" (the standard operating system on the Internet for servers) and "listen on port 113." Port 113 is another standard that allows you to receive DCC, which we'll discuss later.

Popular Tools Internet Travelers Use

Chapter 3

Click on the tab marked "Firewall" and be sure no information is listed there. A *firewall* is a software block created by a network administrator to prevent certain types of communication from going in or out of the network. It would not be present using a modem out of your home. To close this box, click on the word "OK" at the bottom of the screen. To close this box, click on the word "OK" at the bottom of the screen.

At this point, you will only have the main screen up. Click on the icon that looks like a lightening bolt. This will log you on to the default server, which is irc.dal.net on port 7000. As this is the default, it will most likely be busy, and you will not be able to get on. If this happens, click on the icon that looks like a folder. You will recognize this screen as the one where you initially entered your information. Now we're going to concentrate on the top of the screen. You will see a drop menu that reads "random dalnet," with the words "add," "edit," "delete" and "sort" underneath it. Clicking this drop-down arrow produces a list of hundreds of possible IRC servers from which to choose.

Choose another server by clicking on it, then choose "edit." You will see the description of the server, the address and the ports on which to attempt connection. In the ports box, make sure the numbers 6667, 6668, 6669 and 7000 are listed. This gives you four chances to log on to that particular server. Also, by picking a server out of this list, you avoid the defaults, where most other users are logging on, thereby increasing your chances of connecting. Servers have a limited number of people they can accommodate. When you have finished, click [OK] to save the information and bring you back to the screen.

At this point, you can click [OK] again, then click the icon with the lightening bolt or click "Connect to IRC server!," whichever you find easier. If the problem connecting continues, try another server. Particularly if you're trying to connect during prime time

Popular Tools Internet Travelers Use

Chapter 3

(approximately from 5 pm to 2 am Eastern time in the US), you may find most are busy. This is also the period when AOL is busiest, which can also create connection issues within mIRC.

When you are logged on to an IRC server, a box will pop up with a list of "channels" that have been preset in your mIRC client. This list, while extensive, is only a small sampling of the amount and variety of channels available. To get this entire list, close the pop-up box and place your cursor on the main screen. Type "/list," and then get a soda, because it's going to be a while. There can be literally thousands of channels on each IRC server, and it can take as long as five minutes for them all to list, depending on the speed of your connection and the speed of the server. I have seen there be 3000 or more channels on one server, so be patient.

IRC channel list

You may notice when you first log on to a server, the following message: PING? PONG! "Ping" is a way of determining response time between computers. It represents "Packet Internet Groper" and is a diagnostic used to determine if you're connected correctly. "Pong" is the standard response to Ping. Many aspects of the Internet are titled after bad jokes, and of course, "Pong" being the answer to "Ping" is one of these.

If after the ping occurs, you find yourself being logged off, type:

Popular Tools Internet Travelers Use

Chapter 3

```
/raw pong
```

in the main screen buffer and press [Enter] to let the server know you're there and awake when you log back on.

Most servers will not allow you to remain idle, that is, to send nothing to them, for more than two or three minutes. After this time, they determine you are just taking up valuable space and automatically remove you.

Chats are listed by alphabetical order of the name, starting with numbers. After the channel list comes up, you need to join one. This is done by selecting the chat you wish to join, then typing

```
/join #[chat]
```

in the main buffer (see illustration below).

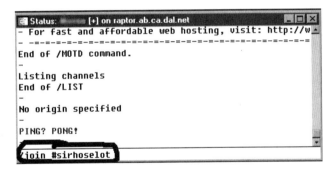

This will move you to the bandwidth occupied by the channel "sirhoselot." After you press [Enter], you will see another window. This one is titled with the name of the channel you selected:

Popular Tools Internet Travelers Use

Chapter 3

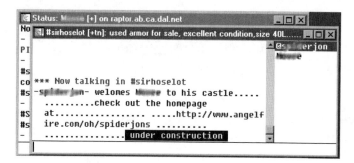

Note that the main window is still visible behind this window. You can manage these windows just like any others. You will remain in the channel you have chosen until you actually close that window or use the command "/quit."

Another way to chat on IRC is similar to AOL's instant messages. On IRC they're called "DCC," Direct Channel Chat. The benefit of DCC is greater than just the privacy of an instant message, however. Servers on the Internet go through a procedure called a split, where one can lose communication with another. If you're on a regular chat channel, these splits can cause lag time in conversation and loss of connection in some cases.

By using DCC, you avoid these splits, giving you a more stable connection. DCC is a function of mIRC, accessed by the menu called "DCC" or the icon resembling a "C" with a lifeline coming from it on the tool bar.

Another function of DCC is to send files via the channel bandwidth, but I'm not going to get into the mechanics of that, since it's not relevant to chatting online. There are many interesting features in your mIRC software, all of which are explained very well by clicking on the icon that looks like a life preserver.

You can leave a channel without leaving the server by typing:

    /quit

Popular Tools Internet Travelers Use

Chapter 3

in the channel's buffer. It is also possible to enter more than one channel at a time, a difference you will note from AOL. The art of IRC is learning to keep track of the main screen and various channels you may enter without lagging behind. This skill just takes practice; start small and work your way up!

To leave IRC entirely, you also type "/quit," this time in the main buffer. You may notice that people who leave IRC have clever or meaningful phrases which display on screen after they leave. You can do this too by clicking on the "Popup menu options" icon and scrolling down to "/quit." The default here says "/quit Leaving!" By deleting "Leaving!" and placing your own phrase, you can change your ending message quickly. As we said before, anything that makes you unique will help you in online chat, since this medium relies on wit and intelligence more than things the eye tells you about people.

The kind of chat you'll see on IRC is not that different from what you'll see on AOL, although the style looks slightly different.

\<Movee\> uh oh, now I can't change it back LOL
\<Barak\> Ahh :)
\<Barak\> -K Dennis
\<Movee\> I have no idea what the Key does
*** Barak sets mode: -k Dennis
\<shyloh\> +k dennis
\<Barak\> =;)

Onscreen, it looks like this:

45

Popular Tools Internet Travelers Use

Chapter 3

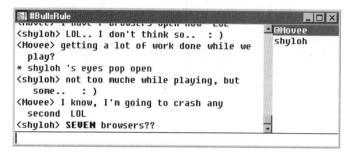

Note the frames of the IRC window, with names of the members in the room on the right and chat on the left, with the chat buffer on the bottom. The "@" next to a name indicates that person is the "Channel operator," the person in charge of the room.

One of the really fun things about IRC is the control the operators have over the room. Don't misuse this control! As the channel operator, you have the power to:

- Remove people from your room

- Prohibit a certain person from entering your room

- Make your room hidden

- Make your room private

- Add a password

- Make it so people can only enter with an invitation

- Ignore people

- Give people the same privileges by making them operators as well

These are all accomplished through the "/mode" command, which is fairly simple to learn, although you may want to make a cheat sheet of all the different addons (called "switches") you can put on

Popular Tools Internet Travelers Use

Chapter 3

it. The mode command is typed into the chat buffer of the channel, just like a line of chat would be. They can only be used by people with channel operator privileges.

Mode commands	
Mode	/mode < channel > +b < nick|address >
Action	ban somebody by nickname or address mask (nick!account@host)
Result	banned user may not return to the area until unbanned
Mode	/mode < channel > +i
Action	channel is invite-only
Result	only a member who is invited may enter this area
Mode	/mode < channel > +l < number >
Action	channel is limited with < number > users allowed maximal
Result	no more than the set number of users may enter
Mode	/mode < channel > +m
Action	channel is moderated, only channel operators and others with 'voice' can talk
Result	good for guest speakers and seminars, prevents interruptions
Mode	/mode < channel > +n
Action	external messages to channel are not allowed
Result	prevents DCC messages from coming from outside the area
Mode	/mode < channel > +p
Action	channel is private
Result	channel shows in listing but cannot be entered

Popular Tools Internet Travelers Use

Chapter 3

Mode commands (Continued)	
Mode	/mode < channel > +s
Action	channel is secret
Result	channel does not show on listing
Mode	/mode < channel > +t
Action	topic limited
Result	only channel operators may change listed topic
Mode	/mode < channel > +o < nick >
Action	makes < nick > a channel operator
Result	grants operator privileges to <nick>
Mode	/mode < channel > +v < nick >
Action	gives < nick > a voice
Result	<nick> may speak and be seen in a moderated room

So, if you were on channel #bullsrule, and you wanted to give operator privileges to someone with the nickname "Jared," all you need to do is type "/mode #bullsrule +o jared" in the chat buffer, and Jared's nick will now appear with an "@" next to it, and Jared can perform operator functions. These commands are not case sensitive; you can type them in upper or lower case, or any combination. Remember that anyone to whom you give channel operator privileges can kick, ban or change your topic, so it's wise to only give them to people you know.

Popular Tools Internet Travelers Use

Chapter 3

Web-Based Chat

Web-based chats come in a few different forms, text and visual. The former comes in two types itself. The one we're looking at is a type of browser, currently available in beta format on AOL.

The second text-based web chat involves going to a site on the web and joining the chats, which is not any different from going to any other URL on the web (one we'll look at is http://www.alamak.com/chat/).

The last type can use a digital camera and allows users to connect to web sites called "Conferences." These conferences are akin to the chat rooms and channels we've already seen.

Electronic Bulletin Boards

This seems like a good time to get into the beginnings of online chat, from where netiquette arose and what it is. IRC and online chat games have existed since the mid 1970s, although they didn't really start to become popular until the early '80s. Then came a surge of electronic bulletin board services, called "BBS" for short. These services offered places to play online games and more importantly, ways to chat with other folks online.

These groups were usually pretty small for two reasons. One reason was that the BBS itself was probably pretty small, being operated out of someone's basement or office with a small maximum number of lines available. Also, users didn't go in via TCP like we do now. A BBS was accessed by something called a "direct dial up."

Popular Tools Internet Travelers Use

Chapter 3

That's how you access AOL now, with your modem, by dialing a number that connects you to a node, which then connects you to AOL. On the BBS, you dialed directly to the service and logged on for a limited number of minutes, set by the system operator, or sysop. To see one of these systems without having to dial in, we're going to connect to one via Telnet.

Log on to your AOL account, then open your Favorite Places icon, the folder in the upper right hand corner. As usual, you need to be using the AOL for Windows 95 version of your software. We're going to create a Favorite Place that will call up the Telnet application resident in Windows 95, then use that to access the Entertainment and Consumers Network.

Click the words "Add Favorite Place." This brings up a dialog box. In the top of the box, in the field marked "Enter the Favorite Place's Description," type "Entertainment and Consumers Network." Tab to the field marked "Enter the Internet Address" and type exactly as written here:

```
telnet://198.211.192.146/.
```

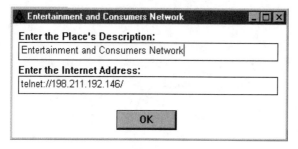

By clicking [OK] here, you have created a favorite place.

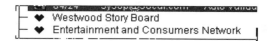

Popular Tools Internet Travelers Use

Chapter 3

Now double-click on that favorite place to bring up your telnet application resident in Windows 95. By following these steps, you'll get an ASCII text-based screen with different messages on it. By maneuvering around, you should be able to get to chats, forums and file libraries.

It looks very much like a primitive version of AOL, because that's exactly what it is. These BBSes are places where people can dial in and chat with a group of people who share similar interests, usually close to their physical locations.

With the use of Telnet, as we've just done, you can now access these smaller boards from the Internet. One big difference to note here, besides the lack of the GUI, is that you're limited in the number of minutes you can be logged on at any one session and during any one month. That's to allow access time for all members.

Telnet looks like this:

```
Telnet - 198.211.192.146
Connect  Edit  Terminal  Help
* MajorTCP/IP by Vircom Inc. *

Connecting...
Auto-sensing...
Auto-sensing PPP...(8 seconds)Hit CTRL-X to abort

Please choose one of these languages/protocols:

    1 ... English/ANSI     The standard English langu
    2 ... English/RIP      The English version of RIP

Choose a number from 1 to 2: 1

              WELCOME!
```

Popular Tools Internet Travelers Use

Chapter 3

Telnet is provided as an element of Windows 95, and you don't need to go through AOL to use it, though you need an ISP. First, connect to your ISP. Then find and launch Telnet.exe (in C:\Windows by default).Then select Connect/Remote System... Now enter the address and continue just as above.

Virtual Places

Now let's explore an enhanced text-based chat tool. AOL's Virtual Places is a browser that allows you to engage in text chat with folks as you surf along the web. Virtual Places is a public beta, which means it is still in testing, so all the glitches may not yet have been removed. To start, you need to go to Keyword VP after logging on to AOL. This will bring you to an area that explains that Virtual Places is in beta and what kinds of things it's going to do for you.

Read this screen, then choose "Accept." This will bring up a short download which will take about 6 minutes, depending on your connection speed. At this point, you will be given an opportunity to choose where AOL installs Virtual Places.

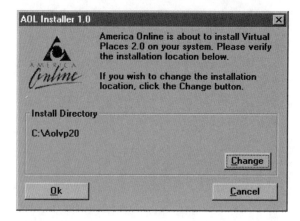

Popular Tools Internet Travelers Use

Chapter 3

If you don't want it installed into the default directory, choose another one by clicking [Change]. As in most instances, the default is the preferred choice. Click [OK] and AOL will install Virtual Places.

When the software is installed, you will need to do the same basic setup as we've done with the other clients as far as filling in your name and other personal information.

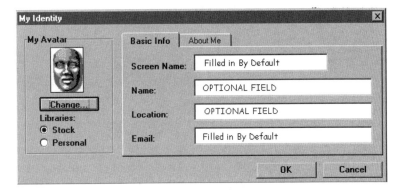

The screen name will be filled in with your AOL screen name and is unchangeable, as will be your Email address. The other two fields on this screen can be filled in at your discretion. You want to click the button marked "Change" under the face and change this picture (called an avatar) to one which better represents you. *Avatar* literally means an embodiment of a concept.

In the case of an online avatar, the concept being embodied is you! You can find these avatars as downloadable files by using almost any search engine on the web and using the word "avatar" as your search string. Leave it at "stock" for now, since you don't have any personal avatars from which to choose. The tab marked "About Me" is entirely optional information, resembling an AOL profile.

You will now be viewing an enhanced web browser like the one pictured below. The squares are the avatars, which are the pictures the users have chosen to represent themselves.

53

Popular Tools Internet Travelers Use

Chapter 3

At the right is a bar listing the people who are in the room with you. At the bottom of the browser is the chat area, where the general room population can converse. Note that America Online must be running in order to access VP. You can get back to VP by using Keyword VP, rereading the notice and accepting the terms each time. It may appear as if AOL is going through the download process again, but this is misleading. The opening screen is merely the same.

Once you get to VP, you can chat with people there by typing in the buffer below the browser, which will cause your words to be displayed on the screen:

Popular Tools Internet Travelers Use

Chapter 3

Virtual Places is not a place you would want to allow children to access by themselves. Also, if you are easily offended by vulgarity or nudity, you may not want to visit there beyond this informational trip. Some of the avatars are of an adult nature, and some of the chat would be deemed unacceptable by most conventional social standards. AOL is working on resolving that to some extent, but for now while it's a beta, use your own judgment about your likes and dislikes.

Web Based Conference Chats

The other type of web chat is pretty straightforward, so we won't spend too much time on it. These are IRC-type chat areas based on web sites. A good one to check out is http://www.alamak.com/chat/, Alamak, in Seattle Washington. This web-based IRC has a clearly identified set of terms you must agree to before you enter the site. Once there, you can engage in the chat one of two ways.

Anyone can log on and chat in any of the areas as a user. The areas are demarcated by a pull-down menu at the bottom of the web site, which has an IRC-type chat buffer with a viewing area above. You can see chat for approximately one minute before the point you arrive, so you can kind of get a feel of how the conversation is flowing and merge more easily. Choices include Teen rooms, music chat, romance chats and even an area called Graveyard. This participation is free of charge.

Popular Tools Internet Travelers Use

Chapter 3

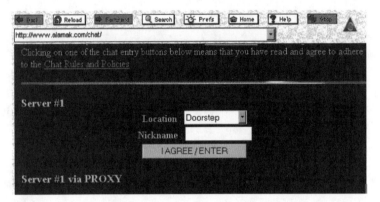

The other way to enter this chat area is with Ops privileges, which are basically the same as the mode commands operators had in the IRC we saw. The difference concerning the user privileges in Alamak is that anyone can chat for free; however, if you want Ops, you have to have an account. It's a small monthly fee that you can set up online with your Master Card or Visa. This account is subject to the same terms of conduct as the free participation and can be revoked if these rules aren't followed.

Enhanced CUSeeMe

Enhanced CUSeeMe is commercial software available on the web or in stores. You can download a trial version of Enhanced CUSeeMe for evaluation purposes at http://www.wpines.com. This is a fully functional version that has a timeout feature, so after the 30-day evaluation period, you have to pay for a registration number to continue using the software or remove it from your computer, as it ceases functioning after the trial period.

Popular Tools Internet Travelers Use

Chapter 3

At this point, we need to be sure you're using the AOL for Windows 95 application. This goes back to the difference between 16-bit and 32-bit applications. CUSeeMe is a 32-bit application, and so needs a 32-bit communications interface.

The way to check is to simply click on the menu marked "Help" on AOL, then choose "About." It will give you a screen that says at the top "America Online for Windows" or "America Online for Windows 95." If it doesn't say "for 95," you need to go to Keyword UPGRADE and get that 95 version.

The download will take you about 35 minutes, so set it up before you log off for the evening, and let it shut down AOL for you. Install it as you installed the previous version, leaving the first version on your machine.

After installation, you can either remove the previous version or leave it on there. I have two versions of AOL on my machine, as I find the 16-bit version works fine for me for most applications and uses less RAM than the 95 version. However, since I need the 95 version for some uses, I keep both. Leaving the 16-bit version on your machine before installing the 95 version will force the installation program to use your previous settings, greatly speeding up the installation and reducing the parts you have to do by hand (like selecting an access number).

Now go to the Start button and again choose Settings/Control Panels/Add/Remove Programs. This time locate the file called "cu21w32x.exe" and choose to install it. When you do so, you'll see a window with three buttons, "setup," "Cancel" and "About." Choose "Setup" here. After approximately three minutes, you'll be presented with another dialog, this one requesting you to fill out an information form.

Popular Tools Internet Travelers Use

Chapter 3

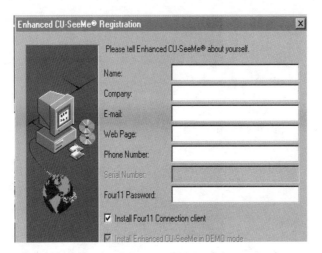

Go ahead and accept the default Install 411 connection client, and insert a password for yourself. Don't enter a telephone number here; this information isn't secure. Web page address is also optional, as is company name. The next dialog box asks which type of setup you want. I always go with the default "typical" here, but you may want to vary that depending on the amount of hard drive space you have.

The directory location options are next. Again, it's best to go with the default here to make it easier to use later. Now the actual installation begins, taking about two minutes. You will be asked to choose the type of camera you intend to use. Just click the button by the appropriate one. This is followed by a request for the type of modem you are using. Unless you are on a network at your place of employment and that's where you are setting up CUSeeMe, choose either the 28.8 Kb modem or the 14.4 Kb modem, which ever is appropriate. We'll actually be using CUSeeMe as a TCP type connection, which you'll see later. Lastly, restart your computer. Enhanced CUSeeMe is now installed.

Popular Tools Internet Travelers Use

Chapter 3

To start CUSeeMe, launch AOL for Windows 95 or connect to your ISP. When you're logged on, minimize AOL by clicking on the line in the upper right hand corner. Now click on Start/Programs and locate "Enhanced CUSeeMe" in the menu, then choose "Enhanced CUSeeMe for Windows" from this secondary menu. Now you're online with CUSeeMe. To call someone, simply choose "conference" from the menus, then scroll down to "call" to find some web sites (called "reflectors") to which to connect. By choosing "phone book," you get a more comprehensive list of these types of chats.

Clicking on "participants" after you get to a site shows you who else is in the room with you. Note that you can only join one conference at a time. Also, if you have logged on via AOL, you may find you have some issues with sending or receiving audio, due to the bandwidth limitations. A 28.8 Kb connection is sometimes insufficiently "wide" to allow audio, which is typically carried in the upper levels of the bandwidth. To circumvent this, you can chat with text by clicking the word "chat" on the Conference menu. You may encounter a message telling you that a site already has its maximum number of users. This is akin to not being able to log on to an IRC server during busy hours. There is no solution for this but to try again or to try another server. This is nothing that the server holders can solve, it's a technology issue.

If you have a friend's IP address, you can add this into the phone book of CUSeeMe by clicking on the "New" button in the phone book. The only way to get a friend's IP address is to ask them, and be aware that many services offer what's called "dynamic IP addresses." This means that the address is different each time they log on. Again, the only way to find out is to talk to your service provider and learn what kind of service you have.

59

Popular Tools Internet Travelers Use

Chapter 3

Videophone

This leads us to the last setup section of this book, the Connectix product "Videophone." This is available from AOL or you can get it from most any computer software supplier. There's also a timed-out evaluation version available at Keyword CONNECTIX, much like the one for CUSeeMe. When you've gone to Keyword CONNECTIX, click on "software libraries," then select "windows library" and locate the Videophone 32-bit demo application, called "CVP-T32."

Same as before, click Start on your toolbar in Windows 95, and select Control Panels/Add/Remove Programs. Locate the CVP file and install. This will install the Videophone software as a thirty-day trial on your hard drive in the directory Program Files/Videophone. You can accept this default or choose to place it somewhere else, as usual. When you've completed the installation, log on to AOL using the Win95 version, minimize it and choose the Videophone icon from the Start menu.

If you click on Settings, then choose Personal Information, you'll see the information you supplied when you installed Videophone. To change this, simply type in the field you wish to change, then choose "Apply." The Apply option isn't highlighted unless you choose to enter new information on the screen.

In "communications" on this screen you'll have the option to either confirm or disable incoming calls, or do neither. I choose to confirm them, because without this feature, you can receive a call you didn't know you were getting if you're working in another application with Videophone or the Videophone launcher running in the background. The Videophone launcher allows you to work in one application without having the Videophone program open. If you receive a call, it opens Videophone for you.

Popular Tools Internet Travelers Use

Chapter 3

If you don't have a microphone, choose Window and click on Show Text Chat to have textual communication like an IRC. This option is also good if you're having trouble receiving audio. Videophone utilizes new technology, and it may take you some tweaking before you can get everything working well.

Also remember, especially when connecting through AOL, you may not have sufficient bandwidth present for audio communication. If you're using a 28.8 Kb connection, and AOL is using some of that bandwidth, you can be left with as little as 26.4 Kb, which isn't enough to carry audio. Making your image smaller will help somewhat, as will reducing frame rates under Settings, and selecting "Frame rate."

When you open Videophone, you'll see this screen:

"Disconnected" in the lower left hand corner means you're not on a call, not that you're not connected to your server. The four sets of digits on the right is your IP address. Remember, if this address is dynamic it changes from session to session.

Like IRC and Virtual Places, Videophone is not currently monitored in any form, which means you can get people on there who are being vulgar or sexually explicit. This is another area that you may want to restrict from children without a parent's supervision. With

Popular Tools Internet Travelers Use

Chapter 3

Confirm Incoming Calls checked in Communications under the Settings menu, you can get a hint sometimes of what type of person is ringing. An incoming call will look like this:

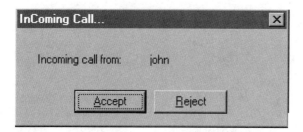

You can choose to accept or reject the call, depending on your whims.

It's easy to find someone to talk to using Videophone. Click on the word File, and choose Call. From here you'll see three options, a personal address book you create, a web server called "411" (which was also installed with CUSeeMe) and the ULS server. Click on the ULS Server tab and you'll see a list of folks using Videophone. To ring any of them, simply double-click their name. Remember, they don't have to accept your call, so it may be a while before you find someone with whom to talk, but be persistent. There are some clever folks out there, sometimes it takes a bit of digging to establish communication!

We're not going to go too in-depth with the visual 'net chat tools, because of the many variables and the network knowledge required to make them work effectively. They both come with excellent manuals that answer most connection questions, and they both are more like talking face to face with someone, since they use audio and visual senses.

Popular Tools Internet Travelers Use

Chapter 3

Helpful Extras

There are a few hardware peripherals you may find handy. We'll talk about those in this section.

Digital video camera

The first is a digital video camera of some sort. Connectix Quickcam is easily obtained and relatively low cost. They also offer superb technical assistance, as well as the videoconferencing software bundled with the camera.

Microphone

Another extra you can pick up at any computer supply store is a microphone, for CUSeeMe and Videophone. In addition, computer sounds called "wavs" are fun and easy to create and share when you've got a group of online friends you know. There are huge subscription lists available via Email that send out 10 or 15 new wav sounds a day or a week, depending on what you join.

Scanner

A third extra that's nice when you have friends you've never seen is a scanner. With this device you can scan photographs of yourself and your life to share online with your friends, which adds a nice bit of humanity. These photos are also nice to add to web pages. With your AOL membership, you have space to create and post your own web page, a great perk. Scanners are also handy for creating pictures of documents, or anything you can copy with a photocopier, so you can take formatted documents and send them to friends and acquaintances without losing fonts and format.

Popular Tools Internet Travelers Use

Chapter 3

Conclusion

America Online chat rooms, mIRC channels, BBSes and Internet video conferencing are examples of the most popular tools Internet travelers use to meet and greet each other. After reading this chapter you should be able to obtain, install and configure these tools for at least basic chat functions.

But as you know from real life experience, there's more to meeting people than just showing up where people are gathered. The next chapter will introduce and explain the social rules that should be followed to keep from looking like a rube to the people you meet online.

Rules

4

Chapter 4

The Written Rules **69**
   Vulgarity 69
   Harassing people 70
   Sexually explicit 72
   Impersonation 72
   Scrolling 73
   Room disruption 73
The Unwritten Rules **74**
Conclusion **75**

Every community or culture has two kinds of rules. Some of these rules are written down; these are the laws. Breaking a law subjects one to a punishment, of which one is often warned before the transgression. Breaking one of the written rules on AOL will cause your account to be actioned and, if you do it enough, canceled. It's the cyber version of exile to Siberia. This is also true with other services which have a written code.

You'll see these codes displayed on your screen when you enter a server in IRC or connect via Telnet to a BBS, and in some places on CUSeeMe a pop up screen will inform you of the legal lay of the land.

This is a sample of rules you might see when connecting to an IRC server:

> Please do not feed the dead, ghoals or vampires.

Rules

Chapter 4

> No bots, File Servers or Clones Allowed.

> We reserve the right to deny access to this server without warning or explanation. By using this server you agree to follow the rules of DALnet.

The other kind of rule is probably far more important and the punishment can be much more harsh, but unfortunately, these aren't written down for reference. These are the unwritten rules of any society, the "don't wear white pants before Memorial Day" rules. They're socially accepted, highly complex and sometimes seem to be completely random. Break one and the consequences range from not being invited to parties to being a laughingstock.

It's no different when you're online. In the online community, however, breaking these rules can net consequences that are uglier than the effect of breaking them in the real world. You can get banned from rooms, get your server banned from other servers, and have your name restricted from newsgroups, in addition to the usual social repercussions. That's why it's so very important to pay attention to the image you're projecting and the culture of the chat area.

> *... it's so very important to pay attention to the image you're projecting and the culture of the chat area.*

Rules

Chapter 4

The Written Rules

Let's start with the easy to identify rules. You can go to Keyword TOS (for Terms of Service) on AOL or read the MOTD (Message of the Day) on the IRC server or the BBS server. Read them carefully and notice what they have in common. This is the cyber version of "No spittin', no swearin'" from the more innocent days portrayed in Westerns, with a healthy dollop of the Golden Rule. So, to put them briefly:

- Don't use vulgarity
- Don't harass people
- Don't be sexually explicit in public
- Don't pretend to be someone else
- Don't scroll the screen so others can't read it
- Don't disrupt the room so no one wants to be there

Now let's take these one at a time. Remember, these are general written guidelines so you need to read the particulars for the service you're using!

Vulgarity

Vulgarity, of course, is somewhat subjective; however, everyone knows that some words are not socially acceptable. These are the words that would get a note sent home if you said them in the fourth grade. They're the things you wouldn't say in front of someone you were trying to impress. They're words that if you heard them at the Academy Awards in an acceptance speech, you'd know you were going to hear about it for years to come. These words are not going to be in a headline of the NY Times.

Rules

Chapter 4

Vulgarity isn't frowned on because the net is populated by a bunch of old-fashioned prudes. Many people enjoy it's easy access to information, regarding it as an enormous worldwide public library, and in this regard, they like to allow their children easy access to it. Allowing their children easy access to rude or vulgar language is not usually on the agenda anywhere.

> *... chatting's purpose is communication. Profane words usually have no relevant meaning and are often used when the speaker can't think of a meaningful term.*

Another reason to avoid profanity is that chatting's purpose is communication. Profane words usually have no relevant meaning and are often used when the speaker can't think of a meaningful term. So, vulgarity doesn't contribute to a worthwhile flow of information, and often it impedes it.

Also, people tend to be put off by rude or vulgar people, so it's just good, common courtesy not to use it with strangers, even strangers whose faces you can't see!

Since your expressions and tone of voice can't be seen online, you have to have other ways to portray your personality in a positive manner, and generally avoiding vulgarity is an easy way to do so.

Harassing people

Harassing people is again somewhat subjective. Are you following them from room to room taunting? That's going to be considered harassment in almost any context. Are you sending them Email after you've been asked not to? Are you continuing a heated discussion that involves the words "You're a___"? That's also harassment. Don't do anything to others that would annoy you or that you wouldn't

Rules

Chapter 4

want done to your loved ones. Some people are more sensitive than others, so judging is hard, but most socialized humans know when they're just picking on someone to bug them.

Remember, too, that no one can see you or hear your tone of voice. In common communication models, nearly three quarters of how we communicate is through posture, tone of voice and other nonvocal cues. With these things removed, you're left with a much narrower scope of information to interpret. What you meant as a casual joke or an ironic statement can come off amazingly bad. Add in the cultural differences of Internet users around the world and it gets worse.

> *Remember, too, that no one can see you or hear your tone of voice. With these things removed, you're left with a much narrower scope of information to interpret.*

I have an online friend I've known online for over a year, never having met her in real life. One day she thought she'd start calling me "convict," an archaic expression referring to Australia's original immigrants. Unfortunately, not being very familiar with that country's history, she had no idea that she was calling me the Australian equivalent of "slave labor."

After a few days, I finally was able to convince her that I was finding the term very insulting, regardless of her intentions. If this had been a person I didn't know very well, I probably would have considered her use of the term to be harassing, and would have avoided contact with her.

If a person to whom you're talking seems to be getting upset at something you're saying, stop saying it. Similarly, if you're being offended by something, don't hesitate to mention it. The person may simply not understand that you're taking offense.

Rules

Chapter 4

Sexually explicit

Not being sexually explicit in public is not as fuzzy an issue. Always remember, these names on the screen are people, just like you. If you're onscreen announcing the measurements of your private parts, you've just done that in front of a room full of people. Would you walk into a crowded high school and drop your trousers or take off your shirt and bra? Probably the fact that you would be arrested would stop you from doing something like that, even if social morals didn't.

There are kids on the net, lots of them, and you can't tell who's who by their screen name, so always act like you're at a formal gathering when it comes to your onscreen chat and sexual innuendoes.

Impersonation

Don't pretend to be someone else. There's only one Mel Gibson in the world. He's a great guy, but unless you're him, don't say you are. That's called *impersonation*, and is a crime if you do it to gain favors or influence. I see about 28 Mr. Gibson's every night and depending on the current sport season, I see lots of John Elways, Michael Jordans and Jose Consecos, not to mention the plethora of television and movie heroes to fill in the gaps.

Your imitation is going to have to be pretty convincing to get past all the rest of the imitators. This kind of thing is anathema in a chat room or IRC situation. When you do that you end up looking like you have no self-confidence, or worse, like a poor liar who thinks the people around them are fools. No one likes to be played for an idiot.

> *Don't pretend to be someone else. That's called impersonation and is a crime if you do it to gain favors or influence.*

Rules

Chapter 4

I've rarely met an uninteresting person on the net, so rely on your own personality to gain friends! You'd be amazed by what you consider to be run-of-the-mill is fascinating to others who haven't been exposed to it.

Scrolling

Scrolling occurs when one sends so much text to screen so rapidly that the remaining text is scrolled off the screen before it can be read, making it impossible to chat. This includes pictures and text. The best way to get attention is to be thoughtful and considerate, not to scroll the screen. Think of scrolling the screen as roughly the same as entering a real room talking so loudly and so much that no one else can chat. It's like being the boor of the party.

Room disruption

The last of these, room disruption, is the hardest to define, but should also be the easiest to prevent. You will find many different beliefs, creeds and persons on the net. You won't agree with all of these.

When does going to a Pagan room and preaching the benefits of B'nai B'rith stop being an interesting diversion and start being disrupting? Mostly, when the person talking has been asked to stop, the room is erupting in personal insults and it's not fun any more. Actually, all of the above rules are disruption of some sort. By paying attention to them, you'll never be guilty of disruption.

Rules

Chapter 4

The Unwritten Rules

So if those are the written rules, what are the unwritten ones? These are the ones that are very hard to define for some people, and have the more severe consequences.

Have you ever been to a party where there was one person who was completely out of place? They ask personal questions, wear inappropriate clothes, talk about taboo subjects and generally make the atmosphere uncomfortable.

Unfortunately, these people are usually totally oblivious that they're doing it. After a while, they may notice that they don't get invited to parties, or when at social functions for work, they tend to be standing alone. This person is ignoring social convention, and the societal response is to ostracize the individual.

> *By mastering the unwritten rules you can go from being a person who dabbles online to a living personality who has real friends and real fun online in the cyber world.*

Very rarely would someone intentionally act inappropriately. Rather, they don't know the standards. However, the written rules are actually evolved from the unwritten ones. By mastering the unwritten rules you can go from being a person who dabbles online to a living personality who has real friends and real fun online in the cyber world.

Rules

Chapter 4

Conclusion

So what is The Rule? I'm sure you've heard it thousands of times in your lifetime, from the time you were in preschool on to present day. Your kindergarten teacher probably had it on a banner over the chalkboard in school. It's very simple: treat others as you would like to be treated.

By leaning on this banal, yet effective regulation of behavior, you will find you rarely break any rule, written or unwritten. By using your own expectations of behavior as a guideline, you can get a good feel for the appropriateness of your own actions. You won't be able to please everyone, but you'll come a whole lot closer!

How Not To Be An Online Embarrassment

5

Chapter 5

Tips On Chatting Well 80
   How to be yourself 81
   Participate! 81
   Type the way you speak 84
   Be conversational 85
   Keep your own personality 87

Ways To Chat Poorly 88
   Personas outside of games 90
   Personal attacks 92

Conclusion 95

Imagine yourself at a casual get together with about 25 folks. Most of the people are milling, talking in small groups of two and three. One person, however, is screaming "Hey! Are you male or female??" at every passerby. Another seems to be masturbating, while a third asks personal questions of women passing by. In another corner, a person is reciting garbled nonsense and loudly repeating, "HALLO! HALLO?" You also see one or two folks wandering through the crowd, asking for directions in broken English. This probably isn't a room where you'd like to spend much of your leisure time.

These people stand out because they are transgressing the bounds of acceptable behavior. These people probably won't find themselves invited to many more social gatherings.

How Not To Be An Online Embarrassment

Chapter 5

Proper behavior is also important when people gather online. Unacceptable behavior will create an infamous reputation for the transgressor and will eventually ostracize one.

The point of this book is to help you understand that online interaction isn't so different than face to face interaction. Things that are not accepted in real life are also inappropriate online. But because online chats are a new forum for most people, you may not realize how your actions are perceived. People who spend a lot of time online recognize an accepted social standard, and you can break it simply by not being aware of it.

As in real life, certain people dress in plaid slacks two inches too short, black socks, white shoes and a striped purple and green shirt, and think they look really sharp. There is an online equivalent who marches into chat rooms without regard for accepted norms and conventions.

Tips On Chatting Well

This chapter will give you some tips on how to chat well or on what constitutes poor chat etiquette. By reading and absorbing these basic tenets, you should find it easy to blend into a group with whom you wish to chat.

Always remember to observe the area's culture before leaping in. Just like the real world where some cultures are based on physical contact and in others touching a stranger is the worst insult imaginable, each chat area is going to have different norms. These tips are for general areas where you'll go mostly when you're first experimenting with online chat.

How Not To Be An Online Embarrassment

Chapter 5

> *Always observe the area's culture before leaping in. Like the real world where some cultures are based on physical contact and in others touching a stranger is the worst insult imaginable, each chat area has different norms.*

How to be yourself

This is really the key to effective online communication: You want to be sure to be yourself. What a strange statement—who else could you be?

But there are some subtle differences in online communication that can make you appear differently than you intend. Here are some things you can do to make sure your personality comes through.

Participate!

When you enter a chat room, say something! No one is going to notice you sitting by yourself being quiet; we can't even see you. If you don't say anything, you may be presumed to be a *lurker*, which is a person who observes chat but doesn't enter into it. The word may not sound complimentary and it's not. A lurker is a voyeur, someone looking for entertainment.

So, what do you say? The answer is simple: almost anything! I usually say "Gidday" because that's what I'd say if I entered the room in real life. Other people say (among others):

- Hi
- Whoops
- \<thud\>
- ::blink:: (we'll go over :: later)
- Hallo
- Greetings
- hugs

How Not To Be An Online Embarrassment

Chapter 5

How do you know what to say? Well, it mostly needs to be you, something you would say in real life. If you would walk into your work place and say "Hi" to your coworkers, say "Hi" online.

If you would wave, wave to folks online. Since there are no visual cues besides the text, the :: characters shown above are one of a few ways to indicate action in an online area. So, ::waves:: would read online as:

    YourName: ::waves::

which is how people will see it online. Another way to indicate an action is to put the action in pointed brackets for the same effect:

    YourName: <waves>

A third way is to draw an arrow with a left pointed bracket and two dashes:

    YourName: <-- waves

which again, indicates that the name at the left is performing the specified action.

Once you've greeted, don't stop! Remember, we can't see you; you have to type on screen to be seen. Talk to people and respond to them. Peppering your chat with actions (like a fine seasoning) will bring life to your chat, making you more interesting to watch than just line after line of unrelated text. But don't make it excessive, like you're suffering from a nerve disorder that makes you twitch and move constantly. Rather, make it natural, every few lines or so.

> *Talk to people and respond to them. Peppering your chat with actions (like a fine seasoning) will bring life to your chat, making you more interesting to watch than just line after line of unrelated text.*

How Not To Be An Online Embarrassment

Chapter 5

You'll be able to get a feel for when it's too much, for example:

YourName:	<winks>
YourName:	<scratches his nose>
YourName:	<gets up and walks around to the back of his chair, stretching his arms over his head and behind his back until he can feel the muscles in his neck and shoulder relax, then slumps down in the chair again>
OldTimeChatt	So how's the weather been out there, YourName?
YourName:	<pauses, tilts his head a second, then responds>

Also, too little action gives less of a feel for the physical you. Somewhere in the middle lies an area where people can get a visual in their heads of the way you move and act, without being inundated with a screenplay-like recitation of your every action.

Remember also that there may be 23 people in the room with you, if not more, and all of them may be engaged in two or three conversations. Online chat can be very difficult to follow, so if you can find a way to work it in naturally, put the name of the person to whom you are responding:

S495Brgde:	Anyone seen the Star Wars home page?
YourName:	S49, check http://www.universalstudios.com.

or:

ParntChattr:	ACK! My son just brought home a toad!
YourName:	Green or brown spotted, Chttr?

How Not To Be An Online Embarrassment

Chapter 5

Type the way you speak

Greetings, faire reader. High and non now tis the time to arrive at that portion of our text which concerns the diction. There may be some notice among thee that the diction contained herein is difficult to read and formalised to the point of unreadable.

Simlarlee, typin' in a distinctlee accented o' odderwise dialectal type iz diztraktin' an' hard to read. So 2 is typng w/2 hvly abbr. txt. Some people go online and revert to kindergarten, with "the" replaced by "da," "g"s dropped from "-ing" words and "dat" replacing "that."

All these variations of online communication defeat the purpose of communicating. By making your type difficult to read, you inhibit communication rather than fostering it. Listen to the way you talk, not your accent but your speech patterns. Do you laugh a lot while you speak? Do you tend to accent many sentences at the end with "you know" or "you see?" Do you have a tendency to speak in short sentences, or change the topic of conversation abruptly. Those aren't flaws, but rather are extensions of your personality, how you communicate with the world. When online, use those same communication techniques:

> *Making your type difficult to read inhibits communication rather than fostering it: Typin' in a distinctlee accented o' odderwise dialectal type iz diztraktin' an' hard to read. So 2 is typng w/2 hvly abbr. txt.*

YourName:	Anyway, so there I was minding my own business when the cop pulls RIGHT up beside me!
ParntChttr:	Your kidding, that happened to my kids, too—unreal.

How Not To Be An Online Embarrassment

Chapter 5

Your emphasis on particular ideas or words expresses who you are to those who communicate with you in a text-based world. Don't deny them these clues to who you are. The more human you make yourself online, the more fun you will have and the more people will want to talk with you.

Be conversational

Online chat is first and foremost an entertainment. You're not entering a business meeting, nor, if you're in a regular chat room, are you adopting a persona or playing someone else. So when you're in a chat room, be conversational! This has a couple of benefits, both for you and for the people with whom you're communicating. First, you don't have to spend a lot of time thinking about what to type next or how to phrase it. Just go as you would in any conversation. Second, it allows people who can't see you to get a better feel for you as a person, which makes it easier for them to get to know you.

> *Make sure your chat is appropriate for the type of conversation you're entering. If the room is telling jokes and being generally lighthearted, don't come in forecasting death and doom or starting a religious debate.*

There are all kinds of conversations, ranging from "how's the weather there?" to solving the world's problems. Make sure your chat is appropriate for the type of conversation you're entering. If the room is telling jokes and being generally lighthearted, don't come in forecasting death and doom or starting a religious debate. Similarly, if a room is having a serious discussion, lighthearted joking might be disruptive.

Conversations also tend to ramble. If you pay attention to how a normal conversation runs, you'll see it's not back and forth, give and take. That classic model of message/feedback works well in forensics class, but doesn't reflect the way genuine conversation

How Not To Be An Online Embarrassment

Chapter 5

works. In the classic model, one person speaks, delivering the message. The receiver hears this message, then responds with feedback: a message of their own. In this way there is a constant flow of information following a logical, structured path.

In reality, however, conversation tend to ramble and wander. What started out as a comment on the music of the Beatles turns into a discussion of Skinner's basic model of reward and punishment, all within a few minutes, depending on how the words struck someone, and how that person reacted:

YourName:	I have a hard time believing The Munsters is classic TV.
NickLuvr:	That "classic" thing is all Madison Ave.
YourName:	Hollywood does those now.
NickLuvr:	I just like the shows.
NickLuvr:	Hollywood does what now?
YourName:	I think "I Love Lucy" is better.
YourName:	the advertisements.

Note in the above example of online chat how the conversation has split into two conversations:

1. Who is responsible for creating advertising.

2. The relative quality of old TV shows.

As you become more adept at chatting you'll learn to carry on four, five or eight hundred conversations at the same time. It's the same kind of shift you would find in a verbal exchange, but with an added time delay. It reads confusing, but when you're actually online in real time, you'll find it makes sense! This confusion arises because the conversation is out of real time, presented in its entirety instead

How Not To Be An Online Embarrassment

Chapter 5

of as it develops. Some people like to send out logs, which are saved sessions of chat. These can be quite confusing and misleading for the same reason the above passage seems confused.

Keep your own personality

All the above is aimed at one goal: transferring your personality from offline to online so you appear as a human and not another faceless entity behind a keyboard. You will find this is the best way to make friends and have a good time in online chat. As I've said before, the online chat world can be compared to a great big bus terminal or train station with hordes of people passing through it hourly. Those people who stand out are the ones who take the time to be recognizable.

There's another kind of recognizability, too, one that most people don't want and that's the clown. Everybody knows a clown. Clowns are the staple of the American sitcom scene. Remember Herb from "WKRP in Cincinnati?" This loser was all things to all people, spending so much time trying to impress Jennifer, the receptionist, that one wondered why he never got fired since he didn't seem to do his job. Another one is Barney in "The Andy Griffith Show." Here was a likable guy who spent so much time trying to be tough that most of the town laughed at him behind his back.

> *There are also people online who are threatened by other people's intelligence or style. The way you'll be able to tell is not if someone dislikes you, but by the people who like you.*

"But Barney didn't know he was a laughingstock! How will I know if I am?" you might ask. In some ways, you won't know, because no one is liked by everyone, even in cyberspace. There's always going to be someone who thinks you're not up to snuff in some respect.

Chapter 5

There are also people online, just like offline, who are threatened by other people's intelligence or style. Those people will find fault in anyone they meet, in order to make themselves feel better about their perceived inadequacies. The way you'll be able to tell is not if someone dislikes you, but by the people who like you.

How does that work? You're going to find that there are groups, almost cliques, online in the various rooms. People will go to the same rooms over and over, and they get to know each other. They may all play trivia together on Friday night, or sit online on Sunday evenings with the television on behind them and watch "X-Files" together, or all join on a sports web chat for Monday night football.

If you find a group of folks who share your interests and meet around you on a regular basis, but isn't accepting you into their group, you may want to be sure that your behavior is not the reason why.

Ways To Chat Poorly

OK, if being yourself is the key to chatting well, how do you chat poorly? I'm not including this as a primer for "snerty" behavior! (A *snert* is a person who disrupts a room or channel either intentionally or unintentionally.)

Rather, I'm including this as a kind of checklist so you can be as aware of what not to do as what to do. It shouldn't contain anything that surprises you or makes you wonder "why on earth shouldn't I do that?" When push comes to shove, it's the Golden Rule, with a few additions.

How Not To Be An Online Embarrassment

Chapter 5

This is a good time to mention that the best way to find out what is and isn't acceptable in any chat room or area is to observe the room to see what the other people are doing. What's perfectly fine in one room is horrifyingly rude in another, and what you can say freely on one channel will bring you an instant ban from another. Observing for a few minutes will give you a feel for the room's flow and atmosphere and save you a good deal of trouble and possible embarrassment! Consider it research time.

> *This is a good time to mention that the best way to find out what is and isn't acceptable in any chat room or area is to observe the room to see what the other people are doing.*

We're assuming, always, that you aren't out looking to make someone dislike you or ban you from a room. There are several different types of bans, known in MUDs as FODs (FOD is an acronym for *Fudge Off and Die*). All are based on parts of your Email address, which is yourname@domainname.com.

You can be personally FODed. That means your screen name is not allowed to log on to the server, but your domain name (the other folks on your server or in your company) retains privileges. You can also be site FODed, which blocks your entire domain name. This means that you have made it so no one else in your site can log on to this server, which will probably upset your co-workers.

There's also a service level ban. Enough people have logged on to some IRC servers from AOL with no knowledge of etiquette that these servers no longer allow log ons from AOL.

How Not To Be An Online Embarrassment

Chapter 5

In the online world, as in reality, we can end up being judged by the actions of our peer group, even though it's not fair to do so. Remember that your actions affect not only you and those you come into direct contact with, but those who are in your peer group as well.

Personas outside of games

Adopting a character role is a major no-no in online etiquette. There are areas online where people play nothing but role-playing games, games where you assume another personality, usually mythological or legendary, and act out a role. It's online Dungeons and Dragons, to name one of the most popular. You'll also find people playing other games called Changeling or Amber or any number of homespun games.

All these games allow you to create a fantasy persona. That's great for a game where everyone has agreed to be someone else. It's not so great when you play with people's minds and perceptions by pretending to be someone you aren't in a room where this is not accepted.

Another pitfall of this particular *faux pas* is you can end up looking like a fool. Remember on the television program Bewitched how Endora used to make Darren look ridiculous by dressing him in period costume while he was in an important meeting or in public? So will you look ridiculous if you go into your local Sears store dressed as Napoleon.

As is the case in so many online dealings, if you wouldn't do it in front of strangers or someone you wanted to impress in

> *Morgana, Ice Queen of Malicahlm, may be a totally fascinating person, but it's a facade ... Morgana is probably not 5'10" with flowing blonde hair, cat-green eyes and the body of an aerobics teacher or a runway model.*

How Not To Be An Online Embarrassment

Chapter 5

reality, you should refrain from doing it online. It's fine to play Duke Atreide, master of Dune, in a Dune role-playing game, but playing him in Men4Romance may get you kicked, banned or ignored. The people behind the chat names are human, just like you, and don't all want to play games.

Keep in mind that it's accepted that people are playing the role of another person in game rooms. Don't get too involved in these fantasies or make them real in your mind! Too often have I seen people decide they are in love with one of the characters in a game room and leave families and friends to fend for themselves while they spend hours locked in a fantasy world.

Morgana, Ice Queen of Malicahlm, may be a totally fascinating person, but it's a facade which was agreed upon when she entered the game. Morgana is probably not 5'10" with flowing blonde hair, cat-green almond-shaped eyes and the body of an aerobics teacher or a runway model. That's an assumed character. In real life, Morgana is probably of average build and average looks, and maybe gets a couple of hours a day to play online when his wife takes her quilting lessons.

Also, you want to be sure when in a chat area that you aren't misrepresenting yourself and playing with people's emotions. You wouldn't want to be talking to someone for months or years and then find out that they were nothing like they had portrayed themselves to be, and you need to treat others with that same respect. That doesn't mean you have to say "I'm plainer than vanilla ice cream," just don't say you're Robert Redford's look-a-like and are mistaken for him in restaurants if you actually have dark brown hair and stand 5'4". You can keep the mystery without being dishonest.

How Not To Be An Online Embarrassment

Chapter 5

Unfortunately, lying about one's looks is prevalent online. It is so bad that an online friend of mine, upon receiving a photograph of me, said with astonishment, "You look just like you said you do!" By being honest in your dealings with other people, you can help change the perception that "everyone online lies."

Your use of words gives you the ability to maintain your mystery, if you so desire, without misleading people. I know a person online who describes himself as "fat, married and middle-aged." This same man can say, with all honesty, that he's 6'3", blond and blue eyed. By choosing which attributes to emphasize, you can control how people visualize you to some extent, without having to resort to falsehoods. If we all looked like Adonis, they wouldn't have written a legend about him!

So, if you're a woman sensitive about your hips, don't mention them; instead focus on your eyes, which you like. If you're thin, describing yourself as "lanky" will put a positive spin on it. Also remember, people's tastes are all different, and what you think is a down point may be the thing to which someone else is most attracted.

Personal attacks

Of all the unpleasant behaviors one can engage in on the net, by far the most obnoxious and damaging is a personal attack, otherwise known as *flaming*.

Flaming is an ugly tradition that is occasionally fostered in some newsgroups and chat areas. The thing to remember, again, is that not everyone is going to like you. That doesn't mean, however, that every comment that you don't want to hear is a personal comment against you.

How Not To Be An Online Embarrassment

Chapter 5

> *Of all the unpleasant behaviors in which one can engage on the net by far the most obnoxious and damaging is called flaming. It's an ugly tradition that is occasionally fostered in some newsgroups and chat areas.*

Comments that begin with "your action," "your comment," "when you did this," etc., are usually going to be responses you can consider constructive. They're guiding comments regarding how others are viewing your actions. Taking them otherwise is demonstrating over-sensitivity and will get you a reputation within a group of being a "lame," or someone who perceives a lot of insult where none exists. Doing it too much is guaranteed to put you on a room's ignore list.

By the same token, you want to be sure you aren't engaging in personal attacks yourself. Watch your text for things that are about people, not actions or topics. Phrases to watch out for are:

```
"You are __,"

"You think ____,"

"You always ___"
```

The first one is a label or an insult or usually both. Calling someone's idea or thoughts "stupid" is in the same category. Telling someone what they think or believe is not a good idea either. Unless you are that person, you don't know what they think, you only know what they say. Finally, generalizations are seldom true. In fact, the only true one I've found is that something is never "always" true!

Instead, try to speak from your own point of view. For instance, make sure you say that a person's actions or words have offended you, not the person him- or herself. This can be done using "I" statements. These are phrases like:

How Not To Be An Online Embarrassment

Chapter 5

"I understand you to be saying ___"

or

"I read that as ___"

and checking for understanding. You may have simply misunderstood!

Also, when talking with someone who doesn't agree with your point of view, make sure you keep your cool. Show your point with factual statements, and refrain from name calling and statements like "it's obvious ___," which invalidate the other participant's opinion. Sarcasm is another form of personal attack which is counterproductive to constructive debate, and may not carry well online in the first place. Instead, say what you mean and say it honestly, frankly and calmly.

Don't get into shouting matches. Typing in all uppercase letters is considering yelling. By typing in all uppercase letters, with lots of exclamation points and typos, you appear to have lost control. You appear irrational. The best way to make a point is to appear to be a person who has thought it through and is talking from their head, not from anger. Think of who you're more likely to consider seriously, someone who seems to be hotheaded and wild or someone who seems to be expressing something to which they've given a bit of thought.

Finally, remember that every person you meet will have a different point of view on the same topic. One of the things that's so incredible about this medium of communication is the vastness of the community and the diversity of its occupants. This diversity is going to be evident in the amazing number of points of view, making it a wonderful place to see how people think and what they believe. By agreeing to disagree, in some cases, you can make good friends, engage in constructive healthy debates and expand your horizons.

How Not To Be An Online Embarrassment

Chapter 5

If you go out to the net with your mind closed to new ideas and new ways of doing thing, you're going to shut yourself out of a great opportunity to grow.

So you go out with an open mind, but find yourself head to head with someone who just wants to tell you that you're wrong. Now what do you do? There's only one solution to this. Some discussions are going to be unresolvable. You may believe in the Christian version of the Bible. Odds are good that if you go to a chat area mostly populated by Jewish chatter, they aren't going to agree with your point of view. If you choose to go to those areas, don't go with the intent of converting them.

Go instead to talk, learn and share, and you'll find that these opposing points of view usually don't vary that much at the core from yours. If you get into a situation with someone who is simply not going to listen to you, drop the subject. Simply stopping discussing it or leave the area. That person probably holds to his beliefs as strongly as you hold to yours, and nothing will be gained by a head-butting screaming match, except a migraine on both sides!

Conclusion

If you reread the above sections, you'll find that chatting well isn't complex or mysterious. Most of the etiquette can be summed up in a nutshell: these are people, just like you, and if you treat them as you would like them to treat you, you won't go wrong.

You don't want someone yelling dogma in your face and shaking their fist at you, so don't do it to them in text form, by using all caps and insisting on your point of view. You would like people to

How Not To Be An Online Embarrassment

Chapter 5

understand the person behind the chat and why you believe as you do, so provide the same courtesy by avoiding name calling and other personal attacks.

You would like people to be honest with you, so be honest with them. It all comes down to mutual respect. A little further on in this book I'll be talking about how to deal with folks who don't feel that need to be respectful to people they meet online. There's a way to do it with dignity and without getting yourself upset and aggravated in the process.

Dealing With Inappropriate Behavior

6

Chapter 6

Types Of Inappropriate Behavior 100
   Attention seekers 101
   Impolite or forward suggestors 109
   Unsolicited mail or messages 111

General Ways To Deal With Inappropriate
   Behavior 116

Conclusion 128

We know that you're reading this book because you would like to be a better communicator online and become part of the great online community. You're interested in other people, making friends and learning new and exciting things.

Unfortunately, this isn't the case for everyone out there. Some folks you'll meet just are not well educated in how to not be an online nuisance and others are there strictly to annoy and disrupt.

I'm going to deal with the unintentional nuisances first, and then we'll talk about what to do for those folks who aren't just being socially unacceptable because they don't know better, but because it gives them a sense of power to ruin someone else's fun.

Dealing With Inappropriate Behavior

Chapter 6

Fortunately, those people are pretty few and far between, and you won't run into them very often. I'll show you how to educate others to be better communicators and how to protect yourself from those that are out to be bothersome.

Let's first look at the different kinds of inappropriate behavior. Then we'll get into what to do if you encounter each of them. There are several distinct categories of poor online behavior you'll be able to spot right off. Soon you'll be able to make it so that they don't interfere with your online chats.

In addition, I'll show you some gentle nudges so you can actually affect these folks and bring them "into the fold" so to speak, and by teaching them, you can learn yourself how to more effectively communicate with people. It's very rewarding to have someone who was being a nuisance become someone who looks to you for guidance, as you go from novice to chat King or Queen yourself. By having patience with these folks and sharing what you know, you can become an enriching factor in their online experience as well.

Types Of Inappropriate Behavior

So, what are the types of disrupters we're going to look at? I group them into three general categories:

1. Attention seekers who disrupt onscreen in the rooms.

2. People who make impolite or forward suggestions, usually in private messages although sometimes in public chat areas.

Dealing With Inappropriate Behavior

Chapter 6

3. Mailers, who send unsolicited files and advertising to Email addresses (also known as *spam*. These folks will be found in all the online areas in some form, and each medium has different methods for how to handle them.

Once you know how to deal with these disrupters, they are only minor annoyances as you chat online. It would be nice if these same tools were available for real life pests as well as those online!

Attention seekers

These are the people you'll see causing trouble onscreen. Lacking acceptable methods of getting noticed, these folks resort to more obnoxious behavior. These individuals use scrolling, harassment and other types of negative behavior to gain what they're looking for: attention.

> *A lot of different behavior falls into this category but it all has one thing in common: it's disruptive, making it hard to hold a conversation around this person's actions.*

What kinds of things will you find this group doing? A lot of different behavior falls into this category but it all has one thing in common: it's disruptive, making it hard to hold a conversation around this person's actions. Look for things that cause the conversation to be stopped or interrupted by one person constantly, but not by monopolizing or "talking over" folks. Mostly, this is going to be activity that doesn't involve the topic at all, rather it overruns the chat area. This behavior will be more commonly seen in the text-based chat mediums, and less often in the visual ones, although it's still possible to have it happen there.

Dealing With Inappropriate Behavior

Chapter 6

Scrolling or flooding

The first and most obvious of these is called *scrolling* or *flooding*. Basically, this is sending line after line of meaningless chat to screen rapidly, causing the screen to scroll faster than it can be read. If someone attempts to send a line of chat while this activity is going on, it is scrolled off before anyone can respond to it. This activity can completely destroy a conversation in very short order. The reason I classify this as possibly not intentional is that there are several ways to achieve this effect, and different types of scrolls.

Scrolling can be done by hand or by computer program add-ons known as macros, which enable a user to program type to be sent to a chat buffer at a single click. This is immensely valuable for such things as greeting newcomers to the area:

| CarolArt: | Hey YourName, Welcome to the room! |
| CarolArt: | Hey there ParentChtr... how are you today! |

writing form Emails that don't require any change but a user's name, in playing online games where the host has no desire to type each question and answer on the spot, but would rather send it in a pre-edited chunk:

Dealing With Inappropriate Behavior

Chapter 6

CarolArt:	~ ~*~*~*~*~WELCOME TO
CarolArt:	DICTIONARY~*~*~*~*~
CarolArt:	~
CarolArt:	~ ~~~~~~RULES~~~~~~~~
CarolArt:	GAMEMASTER SENDS AN OBSCURE WORD TO
CarolArt:	THE SCREEN
CarolArt:	PLAYERS THEN TELL THE 'DEFINITION' OF THE
CarolArt:	WORD (REAL OR IMAGINED)
CarolArt:	PLAYERS ALL VOTE ON WHO'S DEFINITION IS
CarolArt:	THE MOST LIKELY!
CarolArt:	. PLAYER WHO HAS THE MOST VOTES
CarolArt:	WINS!!!

and for making the pictures out of characters and symbols known as ASCII art. These look like this:

Dealing With Inappropriate Behavior

Chapter 6

CarolArt:	.	_
CarolArt:	.	| |
CarolArt:	.	| |===( )//////
CarolArt:	.	|_| |||o o| {S AnyKey}
CarolArt:	.	|||(c) ____
CarolArt:	.	|||\\=/ || _
CarolArt:	.	|||||| || |
CarolArt:	.	|||||| …||____/|-"
CarolArt:	.	|||||| _|_____|_
CarolArt:	.	||| |_____|
CarolArt:	.	||| || || || ||
CarolArt:	.	||| || || || ||
CarolArt:	.	_ _ _ _ _ _ _|||_ _ _ _ _ _ ||-||_ _ _ _ _
CarolArt:	.	|_> || || || || -
CarolArt:	.	Hit Any Key To Continue
CarolArt:		|_____/|
CarolArt:		____/ ==== ____/
CarolArt:		<||_¯\\\\ //¯_||>
CarolArt:		(_Ò | = | Ó_)
CarolArt:		(/ \ )
CarolArt:		\ ø__ø /
CarolArt:		\/||||||\ /
CarolArt:		----

Dealing With Inappropriate Behavior

Chapter 6

As you can see, especially in the case of the artwork, this scroll may be quite entertaining, however, it's a little difficult to chat when a large picture is scrolling across the screen! Someone may be scrolling those pictures, not to be annoying, but simply because they've seen them (or created them) and would like to share them with the group. There are some instances where these pictures may be vulgar, but usually that's from a person who is not an unintentional disrupter.

Another issue with these pictures is that they generally contain a type of symbol called an upper ASCII, hence the name of the artwork. These symbols are actually a font, which is a type of file that displays text on your screen and also allows printers to put text on a page from a computer. In order to see text formatted in a particular type of font, a user must have this file on his hard drive.

The Symbol, or upper ASCII, is not a font that comes installed on Macintoshes; it is a Windows font, which means it's only resident on Windows machines. Your Macintosh, Unix, DOS and other O/S-based neighbors in the chat area you're in aren't going to be able to see this picture drawn with upper ASCII.

> *Another way for an unintentional scroll to happen is if the user has one of these macro programs launched and inadvertently clicks a button that sends a form letter or rule set to screen.*

Instead, they'll get a substitute font, which will not display your picture properly in most cases. The unintentional scroller is usually not aware of this fact either. In this case, it's not only a long string of rapidly sent text, it's also unintelligible, making it even more annoying!

Dealing With Inappropriate Behavior

Chapter 6

Another way for an unintentional scroll to happen is if the user has one of these macro programs launched and inadvertently clicks a button that sends a form letter or rule set to screen. It's usually quite apparent that this has happened and isn't really annoying behavior as much as it is embarrassing to the person to whom it just happened.

Also, be aware that these programs, like any software, can interact poorly with other software that may be running at the same time, and go off seemingly on it's own, uncontrollably.

Again, it's usually pretty obvious when this happens. The good news, for other chatters anyway, is that this kind of malfunction (known as a program error) usually causes the user's operating system to lock up, knocking them offline and forcing a reboot of the system. It doesn't harm the computer, but it does remove them from the chat area by default. This is not a happy moment for the user, but it is a relief for the other chatters!

Be kind if the person comes back, and don't mention it or make fun of him or her. It was something out of their control, bear that in mind. They are well aware it happened.

The next type of scroll is intentional, but it's not intentionally obnoxious. In other words, a person engaging in this kind of scroll is simply trying to get the room to see them, not necessarily disrupt the chat. It can look one of two ways.

The first way is rapid, but short, not the long art macros or the flooding type of activity. It usually looks like the example on the top of the following page:

Dealing With Inappropriate Behavior

Chapter 6

AttnGttr:	H
AttnGttr:	E
AttnGttr:	L
AttnGttr:	L
AttnGttr:	O
AttnGttr:	.
AttnGttr:	T
AttnGttr:	H
AttnGttr:	E
AttnGttr:	R
AttnGttr:	E
AttnGttr:	!

This is disruptive, but usually short lived. The attempt here is to get the room to notice the chat, and was probably preceded by the same user saying the same thing on one line and not getting any response to it.

Another possible reason for this to happen is that the user has seen it somewhere before, and thought it looked nice that way, or devised it on his own, and liked the aesthetics. Usually, this isn't done to intentionally annoy.

The other type of attention getting scroll is usually termed a slow scroll. It's not so much scrolling in that it floods the screen, but it's repetitive nonsensical information sent one line after another, and so fits the definition of scrolling. This scroll looks something like this:

AttnGttr:	*%^$%gft
YourName:	So, we were going to doing the picnic thing next week
ChatLuvr:	That sounds like way too much fun, can anyone come?
AttnGttr:	utytytytyt
AttnGttr:	HGDFHGDF
YourName:	If you're in the area, sure, why not?
AttnGttr:	ituthgtug

Dealing With Inappropriate Behavior

Chapter 6

As you can see, this is not actually interrupting at this point, but can get quite distracting and bothersome if it goes on for any length of time.

Uppercase attention seekers

Another thing an attention seeking user may do is type in all uppercase letters. They don't realize that in online etiquette typing all capital letters is considered yelling. When the shouters chat is not following the topic of the room, and it's being yelled, you can find your patience sorely tempted by this type of accidental troublemaker.

They may be doing it because it helps them see the screen better or they may be doing it because they feel it sets their chat apart from others in the room, much like our one-letter-per-line example earlier. Again, this is rarely done to annoy people and usually casually mentioning that it's considered impolite will be enough to make it stop.

WAV files attention seekers

Another kind of attention seeker is the one who has an interest in .wav files. These files are sounds on a PC, which can also be heard on some Macintosh machines. Using these like you would actions, in other words, sprinkled throughout like seasonings on a dish, is not an issue.

However, some folks get so enchanted with the sounds they can make, in IRC and on AOL chat rooms especially, that they can get to be annoying. Constant repetition of sounds can either drive you crazy with hearing them over and over, or they can slow up your computer's speed temporarily while the software searches for a sound you don't have.

Dealing With Inappropriate Behavior

Chapter 6

As in the case of the slow scroller, gently asking them to stop is usually effective, since this is more likely a person who didn't realize that action was annoying. Sometimes people, in an effort to be entertaining, may not understand they're mostly just being loud!

Impolite or forward suggestors

Although I don't classify this group as "innocent" like the attention getters, they are also not setting out intentionally to disrupt or embarrass. Members of this group just don't recognize that the faces behind the screen names are real people, with real feelings and lives.

These are the people who make graphic solicitations for sex from strangers they encounter online. This can come in the form of an instant message, a private message, a mailing or an outright solicitation onscreen in a chat area. This is the reason I said earlier that you may want to create a gender-neutral screen name to discourage this kind of approach from people.

> *I don't have an adequate explanation of why someone would get online and send "Hey baby, wanna ^$%$# ?" in a private message or DCC chat window to a complete stranger.*

These suggestions can be blatant or they may be hidden behind a "line." Some places online, you may feel like you've stepped back into Saturday Night Fever with people in ill-fitting polyester suits and far too much jewelry and hair styling products strutting up to give you a "hey baby, you look like a Sagittarius to me" at every turn. Although not that pervasive, if you run into a group of them at once, it may seem you're being overwhelmed by these rude strangers.

Dealing With Inappropriate Behavior

Chapter 6

So, how are you going to identify this group? Seems like a simple question, but unfortunately, some of these people think they're smooth and you can get drawn into a long conversation just to find out it's a pick up. The most obvious ones appear as rude or graphic instant messages, private messages or DCC chat.

I don't have an adequate explanation of why someone would get online then send, "Hey baby, wanna ^$%$# ?" in a private message or DCC chat window to a complete stranger so I'm not going to try to offer one. Neither do I have any idea why someone would do it onscreen in a public chat area but they will. Of course, the best thing to do when confronted with this type of approach is to simply close the DCC chat window, close the private message on a BBS, minimize or cancel the IM on AOL and hang up the call on one of the video based media.

The people who think they're smoother are at least a bit more artful. Very rarely will one of them send you a vulgar proposition outright. Instead, these users construct a fantasy to attempt to lure someone in. This is a game for them; it's an ego feeder that you can attract members of the opposite sex with your wit, charm and style. From research, I can tell you that the most common way these lotharios operate is by claiming to have psychic powers and the ability to "feel the pain you have," then offering to help.

The problem is, a lot of folks online are genuinely hurting and this can lead to some manipulative and potentially harmful situations where the person approached may find themselves emotionally overwhelmed, or put themselves in a position of sending money or goods to the solicitor. This type of solicitor will be explored more thoroughly in the chapter on the troublemakers.

The best thing to do when approached by this second type of pickup artist is be alert. Be aware that while psychic phenomenon has never really been thoroughly explored, and you may believe in it or not,

Dealing With Inappropriate Behavior

Chapter 6

there are some genuine charlatans out there. Watch for people who speak in very general terms. Who in this life hasn't had a painful unrequited love from adolescence that still bothers us? Who has never had money trouble? Who doesn't want to be well fed and happy, with a good home life and a fulfilling career? These kinds of things are "sure bets," easy to predict for anyone who pays attention to human behavior.

Remember also that the net is populated entirely by people who have access to a computer and a way to pay for their online access. This means you will run into primarily students and people who are able to be online while their monetary needs are met. It's not a stretch to figure out that a lot of those people will be the part-time employed or stay-at-home spouses of people who work long hours. Someone who can see you're lonely may actually just be savvy that a lot of people online are.

Another reason some people go online is because they lack the social skills or time necessary to have a core group of friends offline. Again, this kind of user is going to be easy prey for the smooth talking pick up artist I'm talking about here. Being alert to the facts that they exist and have easy access to general demographic and behavioral knowledge is the best defense.

Unsolicited mail or messages

This kind of inappropriate behavior comes in several forms, as the previous ones did. There's *spamming*, which is sending solicitations and so forth to a user's mailbox or sending the same message to many different usenet newsgroups.

Another form is sending sexually explicit material to people who have no desire to receive such material. There are also chain letters, sent to hundreds of people all over the net, usually done as a forward and intended to either bring good luck or stave off bad luck.

Dealing With Inappropriate Behavior

Chapter 6

Some people inadvertently end up on a round robin mailing list without their knowledge, finding themselves in a conversation among many people, some of whom they may not know, on a topic they have little interest in. Let's look at each of these and how to make this particular kind of activity stop.

Spamming

Spamming is one of the most annoying things that can be done online outside of a chat area. This term refers to two activities, although they have the same effect. Think of spamming as something akin to scrolling a usenet newsgroup or a user's mailbox. Spamming a mailbox is the same as sending our junk mail to millions of postal customers. These are advertisements for business schemes, get rich quick ideas, single's dating services, BBSes for specific groups, pay-to-join clubs, private Web pages and other advertising.

A user usually gets on this mailing list through no fault of their own or their online service. Rather, the mailers purchase lists from services that create such lists. Some online services do sell lists of their subscribers' email addresses, however, which you can find out by contacting them. If they do so, you can request to not be on this list.

> *Spamming is one of the most annoying things that can be done online outside of a chat area. Spamming a mailbox is the same as sending our junk mail to millions of postal customers.*

The message will usually have a way to be removed from the particular mailing list of the person or group sending the message. However, this is not always effective. The two best ways to stop this kind of annoying activity is to either delete the messages as they come in or to read them, paying careful attention to the headers, which may be at the top or the bottom of the message.

Dealing With Inappropriate Behavior

Chapter 6

It looks like this:

```
──────────── Headers ────────────
From user@domainname.com  Wed May 14 14:55:41 1997
Return-Path: <user@domainname.com>
Received: from maple.cns.net (maple.cns.net [205.132.48.27])
  by emin01.mail.aol.com (8.8.5/8.8.5/AOL-1.0.1)
  with SMTP id OAA19072 for <yourname@aol.com>;
  Wed, 14 May 1997 14:55:38 -0400 (EDT)
Received: from ibm.ibm.net ([129.37.217.227]) by maple.cns.net (Smail-3.2-#7)
  with SMTP id m0wRjD1-000ALDC for <yourname@aol.com>;
  Wed, 14 May 1997 14:55:31 -0400 (EDT)
Message-Id: <m0wRjD1-000ALDC@maple.cns.net>
Date: Wed, 14 May 1997 14:55:31 -0400 (EDT)
X-Sender: user@domainname.com
X-Mailer: Windows Eudora Light Version 1.5.2
Mime-Version: 1.0
Content-Type: text/plain; charset="us-ascii"
To: YourName@aol.com
From: Spam Emailer <user@domainname.com>
Subject: Get Rich Quick!!
```

The first line of the header shows you where the message came from according to your server. There may also be a line called "verified sender," which would be the actual location the mail came from. As you see above, there is no verified sender line, which means this mail was not sent to another server to mask the real sender's name. Most mail will not contain this line in the header.

The next line is the return path. This may be different from the sender, as well, depending on how the message was sent. This line will usually be the same as the line above it. The next line, Received, tells you when the message came in and the IP address for the servers that handled both the outgoing and the incoming message.

Dealing With Inappropriate Behavior

Chapter 6

There may be more than one Received line, depending on how many "bounces" (or servers) the message went through before getting to yours. In the case above, this message was probably sent from a terminal connected to a local area network, a LAN, to a wider network before being received by the server at aol.com.

The SMTP ID is the message. This is the identification of the message itself, which can be traced. The date is the date and time in Greenwich mean time, with the translation to Eastern time provided after it. So, this message was sent 14 May, 1997, at 10:55AM eastern daylight time, and received by the server at aol.com some 7 seconds later.

The X-Sender and X-mailer lines are added by automated mailer programs. In this case, the program is one called Eudora Light, version 1.5.2. If there was a graphic or file attached, it would be MIME encoded by this program, as opposed to base 64 or UUE encoding, which is the purpose for this line. Since no file was attached to this mailing, the MIME type is 1.

Content type is text only, which is indicated on the next line. The character set ("charset=") is the type of font used, which is us-ASCII, the basic set on any computer, Macintosh, Windows, DOS, Unix or any other operating system.

To and From lines are where the mail program will put in the real name of the sender and the real name of the receiver, if known. These lines won't be present if a mail program is not used.

To complain about receiving a spam mailing you need to know the server from which it was sent. This is going to be the return path line. You see that this message is from user@domainname.com. Using the forward function of your particular email setup, send the message, with headers and message intact, to "postmaster@domainname.com."

Dealing With Inappropriate Behavior

Chapter 6

If a Web page is being advertised, you may want to send a copy to "webmaster@domainname.com" as well. This sends mail to the person who administers the servers at that particular domain, who can then take the appropriate action to make sure this doesn't happen again.

Remember to use the domain name listed at return path, and not the one in the line marked "From." "From:" is simply the last place the message was before it got to your server; the return path's information will include the origination point of the message, with any bounces or blocks between here and there.

Please note that some mail programs or servers will hide the headers from your view. This is called "viewruling" or making certain lines invisible in a message. If you receive spam mail that has the headers hidden in this fashion, all you can do is follow the instructions for removal from the list.

In the instance below, the headers have been viewruled, but the message itself contains instruction on how to get off this list. In the instructions are embedded HTML links (like the ones you click on a Web page to reach other Web pages).

Since this message comes from unknown@unknown and is to "you@aol.com," I'm going to get the domain name information by clicking the link, which causes my mail program to start. It automatically fills in the name specified in the HTML link:

> This message was mailed to you as a service of E-Mail Spamming.
> If you would like to be removed from our mailing list <A HREF="mailto:remove@emailspammer.com">CLICK HERE</A>
>
> You will be removed within 48 hours and will never receive any more mail from us. This is an automated removal system.

115

Dealing With Inappropriate Behavior

Chapter 6

By clicking this link, a mail form comes up addressed to remove@emailspammer.com. Change the name Remove to Postmaster and send your complaint on it's way!

Spamming a newsgroup occurs when a person crossposts the same message to many different groups. Remember that some people have to pay for newsgroups by the message and they aren't going to appreciate seeing an advertisement in 17 of them.

If someone spams the newsgroups to which you subscribe, it can be difficult to complain because the original sender's email is easier to conceal. Usually, there's not much to be done about spam in a newsgroup except to complain to the server from where the message originates, which is usually found in the message's headers.

As it's not a form of online chat, I'm not going to get too deeply into spamming here except to say "Don't do it yourself." You not only are annoying a lot of people if you do, but possibly costing them money. That's not a good way to win friends and influence people, and you never know when you may meet them online in a public chat area!

General Ways To Deal With Inappropriate Behavior

In general, each of the different mediums has similar ways to cope with annoying or obnoxious behavior. If gently asking the person to stop the activity doesn't work, you might want to try one of these methods. Remember, in all cases, unless you give out your personal information, these words can't hurt you and they have no more power than the reader grants them. By not taking the words

Dealing With Inappropriate Behavior

Chapter 6

personally, or by putting them into perspective, you will find that most online annoyances are nothing more than words on the screen. Sometimes the best argument is no argument at all.

That being said, the first method of dealing with annoying folks online is to not deal with them at all. This can be done various ways. If you can just ignore it, not responding to the provocation is going to be your first line of defense. Don't give the disrupter the satisfaction of your reaction.

> *Most of these people are looking for approval and attention, and by ignoring their behavior you deny them that. The behavior will only continue as long as it's being rewarded, so simply ignoring it is a powerful tool.*

Like the Pinball Wizard in The Who's rock opera *Tommy*, you didn't see it, you never heard it, not a word of it. Most of these people are looking for approval and attention, and by ignoring their behavior you deny them that. The behavior will only continue as long as it's being rewarded, so simply ignoring it is a powerful tool.

If you find it impossible to ignore the behavior, there is a mechanical ignore you can use as well. On the proprietary services you will usually find a button you can click that will cause the annoying member's chat to disappear from your screen.

In the instance of AOL, you simply double-click the member's name from the "People in Room" list and then choose IGNORE:

Dealing With Inappropriate Behavior

Chapter 6

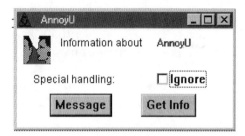

This removes that member's chat from your screen.

Another option strictly on AOL is to call a volunteer member known as a "Guide" to help remove the problem for you. Usually, though, this is only partially effective, as it gives the problem member what he or she is after: attention. By bringing in the cavalry, as it were, you are allowing the problem member to manipulate you, and you're letting him or her know they got to you.

Also, paging a Guide to take care of these issues essentially disempowers you. You now have to trust someone else's judgment that this member was truly a problem. There's always the chance that the problem member will no longer be doing the annoying activity. This is especially true for members who are being annoying intentionally, people who have logged on with the intent to disrupt.

Another way to handle problem members is to report these issues to the service provider. Usually, you can find a way to contact the customer service department of an online service in your literature, or there may be a "keyword" you can use to get there. Cut and paste the offending chat into the appropriate forms in this area.

Dealing With Inappropriate Behavior

Chapter 6

Don't add a note saying "this was very annoying" or threatening the service with lawsuits, cancellation or "do your job" type messages. Just as the people behind the screen names in the chat areas are humans, so are the people who read and take action on logs and clips sent by members in complaint. You may be very angry, and legitimately so, but taking it out on the person reading the clip in the form of a threat or a direct order isn't going to do anything but cause that person to not want to do anything for you.

As someone who's worked customer service for many years, I can tell you that the people who got the most help were the ones who treated me with respect, even when not dealing with me face to face. Always remember in your dealings to treat others as you would like to be treated, and you'll find you get a lot farther than if you try to just talk louder than the other person!

IRC tools: IGNORE

IRC also has tools which you can use to remove problem members from your screen, and in some instances, from your room, even permanently. The first of these is IGNORE, and it works much the same way it does in the proprietary services. Using mIRC, you just choose the user's nickname from the list of people on the channel at the right of the screen. From the menu across the top, choose **Commands**, then select **Ignore User**. This will make the user's chat invisible on your screen. Most of the time, this will eliminate the problem for you. If you prefer to keyboard the command, you simply type "/ignore <username>" in the chat buffer; this will work the same as the menu operated command.

Using KICK

If the person continues to annoy the channel and you are the channel operator, you have two more commands you can use to help dispense with the problem. The first of these is KICK. This command actually removes the offending member from your channel, although

Dealing With Inappropriate Behavior

Chapter 6

nothing stops them from returning. Kick takes the user out of only your channel, so if the user is on several channels at once, only yours is affected.

Don't Abuse Kick! This is a tool to help you remove unwanted troublemakers from your channel. It's bad netiquette to remove users because they aren't chatting about the same topic you are, hold a differing opinion or just have a screen name you don't particularly like. Misuse of Kick can cause the operator of the server to which you log on to ban you from the server, or worse, to ban your entire site.

You will find, as you travel around the servers, that your AOL address will prevent you from logging on in some instances. This is because previous users logging on from AOL have abused the system and made pests out of themselves, and now people using AOL as their Internet provider are no longer welcome on that server. AOL is by no means alone in this, so always keep in mind that your actions affect people all around, even folks you never meet.

To use KICK, simply click once on the user's name on the list in the right side of the screen. Select the menu called **Command** from the top of the screen and choose **Kick user**. This will close that user's connection to your channel, removing him or her until they choose to rejoin.

Using BAN

If you've kicked the problem member and they continue to come back and disrupt the channel, you may want to consider using the most powerful tool in your arsenal as a channel operator, that of BAN. Ban is operated from the menu across the top called **Command**, the same as the previous two commands. Again, highlight that member's name and choose **ban user**. This will prevent that user from rejoining your channel until such time as you unban them.

Dealing With Inappropriate Behavior

Chapter 6

Banning, like kicking, should never be misused or abused. This is for the same reason that Kicking should never be abused, mainly, it's poor manners and can get you as well as your site removed from the welcome list on the server to which you log on. To BAN with a keyboard command, simply type:

```
/ban <user name> <channel>
```

in the chat buffer. Doing this after you have kicked the member is going to be the most effective use of this command.

To unban, you simply double-click the chat area on the mIRC channel screen. This will bring up a dialog box with options to do such things as setting modes for the room and viewing the ban list. To remove anyone from the ban list, simply delete their name. It should be noted that these commands can only be changed by the channel operator at the time, although they can be viewed by anyone in the room.

So you've ignored, you've kicked and you've banned and the problem member keeps coming back. Now what do you do? If you recall, when you first log on to the server with an IRC chat program, you are usually presented with the MOTD, the message of the day. If you read this message carefully, you should find something like the following contained within it:

> - All matters regarding this server should be addressed to strahd@dal.net
> - Visit our server's homepage: http://barovia.dal.net
> End of /MOTD command.

The first line here tells you the email address of the server's administrator, the sysop. To report a repeat problem member, you would send mail to the address listed.

Dealing With Inappropriate Behavior

Chapter 6

Don't expect the sysop to take care of the issue for you! The proprietary services are being paid by you to take care of such issues, but the systems administrator on a private server most likely is not. This is not to say you shouldn't try this route if all else fails, but don't go into it expecting that your complaint will be acted on. Another truth of the Internet is that it's very big, and most of the time you're on your own.

While this has the plus side of making it much freer and easier to exchange information and ideas, the down side is that you have to provide your own security and bouncers in most cases. We'll go over in-depth the ways to do that later in this book.

Web-based chats, for the most part, have the same kinds of self empowerment tools that IRCs have. Again, depending on whether you're logged on as a channel operator or a nonpaying chat member, the types of tools at your disposal vary. If you're using the free access route, without a subscription to the web-based service, you'll find that mostly you need to learn to ignore people. There is always, of course, the option of writing to the server's administrator, the same as with an IRC. However, if you choose to pay for the service, that's an entirely different thing.

When you pay for the monthly subscription to most Web-based servers, you are actually paying for channel operator privileges. This means you have access to Kick, Ban, Ignore and other functions. Channel operators not only have the tools to remove unwanted users, but they can also make the rooms hard or impossible to access and themselves hard or impossible to find.

For instance, using MODE, one can turn his or her room into a private room, which means it's not listed by the **List** command, nor will it appear on the server's pull-down list of rooms from the main public area. You can also make yourself invisible to anyone who

Dealing With Inappropriate Behavior

Chapter 6

doesn't know the exact spelling of your name, which is handy for getting people who decide they want to have a personal vendetta off your back.

Change your screen name or nickname

Another way on a Web-based chat, or indeed on an IRC or proprietary service, to get away from people who are engaging in personalized types of unacceptable activity is to simply change your screen name or nickname. By so doing, and then only updating people who you consider to be your friends and trusted acquaintances, you can cut down on such things as email and IM message harassment. Sometimes the best offense is a good defense, to quote the sports world!

From this, you can see that it might be money well spent to get channel operator privileges on Web-based chats. This allows you, once again, to empower yourself, instead of having to rely on someone else taking care of it for you. By doing this you are able to control your own chat experience, and not be at the mercy of people who have the urge to disrupt, or people who don't have the same standards you do.

Also, by being able to handle these problems yourself, you will probably find chatting to be less frustrating. No one likes to feel like a target, and when you are the channel operator, or have the channel operator privileges, you aren't a target. It's always better to be part of the solution.

Inappropriate behavior and visual-based mediums

The final place where you may run into issues with inappropriate behavior is going to be in the visual-based mediums, like CUSeeMe and Videophone. Unfortunately, since this is a one-on-one chat, the behavior you find exhibited is going to be more offensive, in most cases, than you will find on a text-based chat. That's because text

Dealing With Inappropriate Behavior

Chapter 6

based chat is just that: text. There's no way to really show you anything private or gruesome or in bad taste, because it's all just words. I won't even attempt to explain why some people, given a digital camera, will aim it at their private parts and performs acts of a public sexual nature, sometimes aiming them at people who aren't in any way indicating they're interested.

My general take on this type of behavior is that if you want to do that and the person viewing wants to watch, then there's no reason not to do so. As long as it's not illegal, and you're not forcing it on anyone else, that should be the kind of thing left up to personal taste. However, when you're making someone else watch it, or you're just doing it randomly in hopes the person on the other end will be interested, then there's a problem. So, how to prevent this from being done around you? Well, let's look at some.

First, you can block all incoming calls on most video-based chat mediums. To do this with Videophone, simply select **Settings** from the pull-down menu, then choose **Connection**. That will bring up a dialogue box, where your modem and TCP/IP selections are checked. Under those you will see two check boxes. One of them reads "Confirm incoming calls" and the other reads "Disable Incoming Calls." These are two manifestations of basically the same thing. They both give you the opportunity to prevent an unwanted call from ever occupying your screen.

Before disabling incoming calls, however, I would first try confirming them. This will give you the ability to "screen" your calls, to let you know immediately if the caller is someone you know or if it's someone with whom you might be interested in talking. It will also give you the ability to see right away if it's someone who is being open about their intentions to perform sexually in front of the camera.

Dealing With Inappropriate Behavior

Chapter 6

If you're not interested in having that done, you can simply click to refuse the call from "HotLover," "SexyNHot" or "Ready4U." On the other hand, the downside of this semi-block is that there are people who want to act inappropriately who don't care if the person on the other end is interested in that activity and therefore take pains to hide their intention.

This happens in two ways. One way is the person's screen name will seem very ordinary. You get a call in from "Joe," you choose to accept because you see nothing wrong with Joe's personal information after looking it up on the ULS server, and he lives in an area you are interested in going to for holiday, let's say. When Joe comes onscreen, however, you've got a shot of his privates, which is the last thing you were expecting.

This can be shocking and upsetting, to say the least. What can you do here? Hang up. The ULS servers are at this time unregulated, and it's a private transmission, which means it's not violating any current laws, so far as has been proven as of this writing. There's no real action the ULS server's administrator can do, as it's publicly accessed by groups who purchase the software, and unverified.

If you get angry with Joe and say something huffy into your microphone or if you type something huffy on the text chat buffer, you may be feeding his ego so he continues this behavior. The only way to make it stop is to stop it yourself by disconnecting the call. This doesn't mean Joe won't call back, but now you know his name, and you know not to accept the call. Try to remember in these instances, you are a victim and you need to take control of the situation to stop the victimization.

Dealing With Inappropriate Behavior

Chapter 6

Another way to protect yourself online with a visual chat medium is to change the personal information in your connections setting to something not gender specific. Most victims of the sexual call are female and that's what is being sought out on the ULS server by the people doing the inappropriate activity.

Change your name to something neutral (for example, use just a first initial, only initials or even assume a name) to discourage them from ever calling you. If you opt to go with an assumed name, again, make it something gender neutral. Not much is going to be gained by switching from Kathy Smith to Lady Kath if you're trying to dissuade rude callers! Changing your personal information to read K. Smith, or K.S., or BookLearned, however, might be enough to keep folks away from you.

I call this method "The Club," after the car theft deterrent tool. While the tool itself is an effective means of keeping your car from being stolen, it's primary value is in it's bright red color and easy visibility. This coaxes the car thief into taking the car next to yours that doesn't have a big heavy metal stick across the steering wheel and is much easier to steal! The Club method won't stop all calls but it makes them less likely.

So you've tried selectively screening calls, but too many Joes are getting through, so you decide to disable all incoming calls. This works, but also has its downside. You can make outgoing calls, which means that you can surf the ULS server and look for names that look, through their location or comments, like they might have similar interests to your own. You can call them and chat with them with all your incoming calls disabled.

However, if someone is doing the same thing, surfing the ULS server, and thinks you sound interesting, you're going to miss out on that call. At this point, you have to ask yourself which is the better risk,

Dealing With Inappropriate Behavior

Chapter 6

occasionally getting a Joe, or missing out on a call from someone you might find very interesting and maybe losing the opportunity to make a friend.

You can also add comments to your personal information that make your reasons for being online clear. There is a section, when you click on **Settings**, then **Connection**, on the Personal Information tab, where you can put a short sentence or blurb.

This is also a place where you can have a lot of fun! I was once in a group of people who all enjoyed food from Taco Bell. One day in a busy moment, we were exploring the visual mediums and playing with this comment area on our own personal information. We all said that we had Refried Beans installed on our computers. Some people had comments that they had the revised Refried Beans version 2.1, others put that they had Refried Beans for Macintosh, and so on in this vein.

Before long, the ULS server was dotted with people who had Refried Beans. As the minutes passed, soon information started appearing from people who were not in our group but who were also playing the Refried Beans game. One person in Oregon was looking for the update to Refried Beans called Shredded Cheese. Another person in Delaware posted that although they had no Refried Beans, they did have special gaming codes to Tacos. Community interaction and idea development like this are the reasons that online chat is worth the risk of getting the occasional unacceptable call.

Another way to protect yourself, which is similar to disabling all incoming calls but allows folks who know you to ring is to not register with the ULS server. To do this, you simply have to uncheck that option when you launch the camera linked application. Again, the downside to this is that you may miss a call from someone who shares your interests and with whom you might possibly have a great online friendship.

Dealing With Inappropriate Behavior

Chapter 6

However, it does stop people who are surfing the ULS server looking for victims from finding you easily. Whether this risk is more or less important is a decision only you can make.

Conclusion

We've looked at the kinds of disruptive behavior you may find online in a chat area and what kinds of things you can do to stop it. We've also discussed how to prevent it from starting to begin with, and a bit of the reasoning behind it. We've also looked at how the online medium can be rewarding despite it's occasional troublemakers.

It's easy, in a chapter focusing on the "bad seeds" to feel like the net is populated with nothing but troublemakers and people who hold different sexual and moral values from our own. Nothing could be farther from the truth! If the net was nothing but hoodlums and pests, there would be no need for a book on online chat.

Fortunately, the troublemakers are few and far between. By being prepared for them, you can prevent them from spoiling your fun while online in a chat area. Consider it sort of like a vaccination from disease you get before going on an international trip. It might be easy to think that the world was crawling with deadly germs, when in fact, the vaccination is merely to prevent the possibility, not to emphasize the probability.

You would miss out on a lot of interesting places and people if you let the perception that you would be attacked at every turn by deadly germs stop you from going anywhere.

Who Are These People, Anyway?

Chapter 7

Why Do People Chat? 132
   So what's the answer? ....
   Why do people chat? 132
   Meet people 136
   Games 138
   MUD (Multi-User Dungeon) 141
   Safe forums 155
   Resources 158
   Red light district 161
   Romance 164
   Support 165
Conclusion 166

So who are the folks you meet online? Some of them are annoying pests, we know that already from the previous chapter, but what about the others? If 10% of them are people out to disrupt, then 90% of them must be there for another reason.

First, I'm going to go over the kinds of people I have observed online and the reasons they give me for why they're there. In this way, I hope to provide, not scientifically deduced proof perhaps, but at least anecdotal clues about who these folks are and why they're here. To paraphrase Dr. McCoy from the original *Star Trek* series "I'm a writer, Jim, not a psychologist." However, I can still relate what I've seen and let you draw your own conclusions.

Second, I hope to be able to give you some hints how to communicate with people who are online for particular reasons. You

Who Are These People, Anyway?

Chapter 7

can be a force for great good if you can lend a caring ear and a kind word to a lot of the folks you'll meet online, maybe even more than you realize.

Why Do People Chat?

This is the question that is the hardest to answer when I'm approached by people who've never been exposed to online chat. They're curious about why I would spend hours talking to people I've never met, what the fascination is for cruising the chat rooms looking at profiles and starting conversations with strangers. They hear horror stories about the shadier figures who visit the net and get sensationalized on the evening news for their criminal activities.

So what's the answer? Why do people chat?

To answer this question, first we have to look at who these people are. The answer may surprise you! To get this information, I conducted an informal survey of about 300 people I either know or I saw and approached blindly. This is what I found:

- ❖ Most of them are self employed. They make enough money to own a computer and maintain an Internet connection of some type.

- ❖ A good many of them are students at universities around the world.

- ❖ Most of them are women.

Who Are These People, Anyway?

Chapter 7

- About half are married, between the ages of 35 and 45, and have at least one school-aged child.

- A great many of them suffer from a debilitating illness or phobia that prevents them from going out much.

- A few are house-bound, using the net as their sole connection to the outside world beyond nurses and family.

- Some of those surveyed listed professions of online service management, housewife, mother, web page designer, police officer, writer, chef, software support technician, secretary, manager, production line worker, lawyer and photographer.

- They live in large cities, small towns, remote areas and suburbs, inhabiting dormitories, apartments, studios, town houses, condominiums, houses and cabins.

- Some have offices, some use a corner of the basement, some have part of the living room, dining room or den. One woman has her desk set up in a large closet in her parent's house.

- Many of them have cats, many have dogs, a few have parrots, one has a pot-bellied pig.

- They share their yards with deer, raccoons, rabbits, gophers, prairie dogs, skunks and elk from time to time. Some garden, some have xeriscapes, some have professionals come and tend their lawns, while others slave over a hot lawn mower once a week. Gardens grow vegetables, flowers or sometimes both; some people grow most of the food they eat, others just cultivate flowers to decorate their homes.

Who Are These People, Anyway?

Chapter 7

- Some of them have enough money to live comfortably, and some scrape by with just enough to pay the bills and eat. Most are somewhere in the middle, with enough to be stable, but always kind of on the edge.

- They all love games, online and offline and play them quite a bit with friends and groups.

- They all share a love of people and a sense of belonging somewhere online.

- They are all of different ethnicity and color.

- Some love basketball, others are diehard hockey fans, some cannot get enough of baseball and most enjoy football. Some had played football or run track at school, and now have children in the same sports. Others enjoy fishing, and a few hunt for sport.

In other words, the people you meet online are the people in your neighborhood, workplace or favorite hangout. There's nothing unique about the members and users of online services or other types of chat. They're just people, like you and me, trying to make it through the best they can with what they've been given. They've chosen to do some of that with online interaction, learning about folks around them.

> ... the people you meet online are the people in your neighborhood, workplace or favorite hangout. They're just people, like you and me, trying to make it through the best they can with what they've been given.

They've also decided, in addition to learning about others, to learn something about themselves, too, in most cases. They better themselves with classes online and with web surfing for hours, learning how to do things for themselves and better themselves. In addition, they like to put up web pages of their own, teaching others

Who Are These People, Anyway?

Chapter 7

how to do things they feel they're particularly good at, or just sharing pieces of their lives with folks. On many occasions, you can enter an IRC channel and get dozens of URLs to interesting web pages people share.

Now that we know who they are, let's think about why they're here. This is the detail that, if you can get a handle on it, will help you more than anything else when you deal with people you meet online. In any situation, knowing a person's motivation is the key to understanding that person's behavior. In fiction writing, there's a formula which says "Plot is action and action is motivation." What it means is that if you know a character's motivation, you know how that character will act in any given situation, allowing you to write more believable characters.

For instance, suppose Johnny never felt like his mother accepted him for who he was, always wanting him to be better than his big brother Rick. Now that Johnny's grown, he may be the kind of person to take on too much work in hopes that it will cause people to admire him for his deeds. Another possible reaction is that Johnny may agree with everyone he meets, dreading confrontation and the idea that someone doesn't approve of him. He may hide certain actions if he feels they are "selfish" or "bad." He may end up doing a lot of things he doesn't want to do because he feels he "should" do them. He may be eaten up with guilt at not wanting to do these things. If you know why your character of Johnny is behaving the way he is, you can make him become a real person on paper, because he reacts like we react, and we can identify with him.

Similarly, online we may run into the same kind of people we were writing about with Johnny. They may do things that seem, at times, inexplicable. The only way to find out why these people are behaving this way is to get to know them, to talk to them and share with them. They may be completely dumbfounded at some of your beliefs and actions as well, always remember that.

Who Are These People, Anyway?

Chapter 7

Let's think about the action of logging on and entering the online chat world. What are some of the reasons that people start to do that?

Meet people

One big reason is that it's an excellent place to meet plenty of people who share the same kinds of interests as you do. With the net and online chat you're no longer limited to the local library's listings of clubs who meet in their conference rooms. You don't have to join a society to get notices of meetings, you don't have to attend meetings at all. You can have an ongoing, 24 hour a day meeting on a message board in a newsgroup on the Internet. If you take this same accessibility and add to it the ability to chat in real time with real people, you have an unbeatable combination.

Suppose you were a writer and you needed to know what kinds of things a pilot is trained to do in the event of an airplane crash. A few years ago, you would have had to find a pilot, probably in the yellow pages unless you were lucky enough to know someone who was a pilot or knew a pilot personally. Then you'd have to meet with that person at a time when you were both easily accessible and interview them. The other option would be to guess. You could read a piloting book, perhaps, to get the technical details correct. Beyond that, it was pretty much a lot of legwork and guess work.

Now, thanks to the web, your job would be much easier. You can surf the web to find articles from plane crash survivors, read technical data and black box information. Then, you can go to a live interactive chat room with a topic called Pilots Who've Crashed. You can talk to real live people, right then, and more than one viewpoint will be offered. Maybe there's even some debate about which procedure is actually correct, or there's a controversy that's been brewing about one particular regulation that you didn't even

Who Are These People, Anyway?

Chapter 7

know existed. You can pick up the lingo and technical jargon, and get a feel for the real life dialog between tower and pilot without ever leaving your chair.

Another example would be if you were very interested in AIDS research but you live in an area with very few resources. By logging on to your local ISP or IRC server, you can find literally hundred of rooms with thousands of people who are interested in AIDS research. You can talk to people who have the disease. Better, you can interact with them on a human level, find out what it's like to live with that disease. You can find out what kinds of treatments they take, how they make them feel and what you can do to help. In this way, you can not only better educate yourself, but you become a carrier of that knowledge. The more people know, the better prepared they are to deal with life and the world.

How about gardening? Ever wondered how expert gardeners get those tomatoes to grow just right? Join a forum chat on a proprietary service about gardening. How about quilting? Genealogy? They're all here in channels filled with people who want to learn and share. People who are online in those types of channels have chosen them because that's where their interests lie, and all different skill levels gather there. It's like an information orchard with fruit waiting to be picked.

Another reason people chat online is to find others who want to learn what they know. This is the other side of the previous group. Now we're talking about folks who have the knowledge and want to pass it on. This is not unlike the storytellers of yore who gathered folks around the fire to talk to them about legends, myths and lessons. Online is a great forum for this kind of activity. You don't need a license, you don't need a text book, and you have students who are volunteering to learn. While everything these folks say may not be right, it's usually pretty interesting, and if it's not, there's always another 1,756 channels to look into!

Who Are These People, Anyway?

Chapter 7

Games

One of the common interests people share online is a love of games. If you recall, in my informal survey everyone answered that they really enjoyed games of all sorts. One of the online wonders is the ability to play all sorts of games that aren't possible to get into to such a degree in real life. For instance, in poker games you can play with people from all over the world, at the same time. Many of these web sites which allow interactive gaming also have chat areas so you can talk while you play. I have a few words of advice here too, for people playing in those games.

> *One of the common interests people share online is a love of games. One of the online wonders is the ability to play all sorts of games that aren't possible to get into to such a degree in real life.*

Suppose you're playing poker, since that was the example above. Don't announce you have a great hand before the turn is over! That isn't appreciated at real life games and the people online aren't going to like it either. It also marks you as a rube, not a good label.

Take the time to read the rules of the game you're playing. With games like poker, bingo, slot machines, hearts, etc., you usually have to download software from the web server that will allow you to connect to the game. This software will come with instructions not only for set up, but also the rules of the game (or games, if it contains more than one). Little is more aggravating when you're trying to concentrate on a game than having to stop and answer questions when the answers are easily available in the help file. Reading the rules will not only help you not be annoying your first few times playing the game, but will also make the game more fun for you.

Take some time to watch a few rounds of the game if possible. Some web games will allow you to *lurk*, which is sitting in the room but

Who Are These People, Anyway?

Chapter 7

not actually participating. Taking advantage of this will allow you to see what the culture is like in this particular game.

For example:

- ❖ Do they chat a lot?

- ❖ Is it mostly confined to bets and compliments or is there friendly banter and chatter?

- ❖ Do the folks seem to know each other?

Taking the time to determine these will also make the game better for you. Once you've sat out a few rounds and observed, get into the game but don't become a pest. Play and see how you're accepted, see if anyone wants to be friendly to you. Some of these groups have been playing together for weeks or months and a newcomer may be viewed with a wary eye for a little bit. Make sure it's obvious your intent is to play and have fun, not dominate or disrupt.

If you're truly puzzled about a rule, don't hesitate to ask about it after you've read the documentation and looked for an answer. Some documentation is not clear and most folks are more than happy to help with the more difficult things.

I remember the first time I was playing a game of poker called Omaha Hold 'em, which was a game I'd never seen before in real life. It involved dealing a hand of four cards from the computer to each player, which only that player could see, then a round of bets, then the computer dealt three cards to a common hand, that everyone could view. Another round of bets followed, then another card we could all see, then another round of bets, then another card.

I noticed that as each hand was dealt, then each subsequent card, a card would be thrown under the gathering pile of chips in the pot. I checked all over the documentation, and could find nothing about why this was being done.

Who Are These People, Anyway?

Chapter 7

Finally, I excused myself to the group, which was rather quiet and asked if anyone knew why there were cards under the pot. Several people admitted they didn't know, then one person explained it was to imitate real Las Vegas style poker, where the dealer will do that to prove he's not dealing from the bottom of the deck. It was just a touch of realism to add to the game.

In that case, it was a valuable question, because several other people at the table who maybe had noticed it but weren't curious, or who hadn't noticed it at all also got the answer to the question.

In addition, my chatting eventually changed the tone of the group a bit, and they became much more vocal. It was very soon not unlike being gathered around the card table for a casual game with the neighborhood folk. This group meets pretty regularly, and it's fascinating to share in their lives. They talk about their day, their kids, what they had for dinner. It's very down home and comfortable.

> *An important point to remember about online games like these is that you can't force anyone to like you or to talk. Work with the culture in which you find yourself instead of forcing it to adapt to you, it will go much easier.*

An important point to remember about online games like these is that you can't force anyone to like you or to talk. Some people prefer to play their games quietly without a lot of onscreen chat. Others really enjoy a good conversation about last night's dinner while playing Hearts on the web. If you try and work with the culture in which you find yourself instead of forcing it to adapt to you, things will go much easier.

Who Are These People, Anyway?

Chapter 7

Conversely, if you find that you're having to alter your personal style too much to fit into the group, perhaps you should play at another table or choose another game. The point of gaming is to have fun, which no one is doing if there's a lot of stress and awkwardness at the playing station.

This pretty much holds true at any level of online chat. There's a certain amount of adaptation that has to take place, no one really ever slides right into the hole without a little bit of sanding! There's a limit to how much either side should need to give, though, before it becomes apparent it's just not a good match.

Fortunately, the online world is huge, and if one group doesn't work out, there's always another that will, it's just a matter of finding it. I move around a lot while I'm online, through various circles and forums, because I enjoy meeting new people, and staying in your own little group isn't a good way to do that. By branching out, you find the best and worst in folks, and you can go from there.

MUD (Multi-User Dungeon)

Card games and board games aren't the only games you can play online. MUDs, in fact, go way back to the late 70s and the early 80s. The first MUD (Multi-User Dungeon) was created in 1979 by Roy Trubshaw and Richard Bartle at Essex University. These imagination-fueled games were and are still completely unlimited by anything but the MUD builder's imagination.

Some other terms for MUDs are:

>MUSH (Multi-User Shared Hallucination)

>MOO (MUD Object Oriented)

Who Are These People, Anyway?

Chapter 7

These fantasy games are the heart of the online gaming world and the real beginning of interactive online chat. When DOS and UNIX were the main operating systems, and Windows not even a gleam in Bill Gates's mind yet, virtually no one had heard of richly graphic PC video games.

A fast modem would connect you at 300 baud (compared to today's 33,600 standard), so these games were mostly housed on large mainframes at universities and were mostly built, populated and managed by students when they weren't in class. Instead of a graphical interface, these games are text based, leaving the images of the world you've entered in the user's mind.

Using a MUD

The MUD we'll look at is *Dragon*, situated via telnet at jgsdos.brooktrout.com. Again, to use Telnet, you'll need to be using the 32-bit version of AOL (the one for Windows 95).

Enter this telnet address in your Favorite Places folder by opening Favorite places, then choosing Add Favorite Place. For description, type:

    Dragon

For Internet Address, place:

    telnet://jgsdos.brooktrout.com

Clicking OK here will create a heart. Double-click the heart to launch the World Wide Web browser. As soon as the browser comes up, Telnet will also launch.

At this point you can close the browser in AOL. To telnet to a MUD without using AOL, first open your ISP connection. Next, find and launch the telnet program. If you are using Windows 95, use the start menu's **Find** command to locate Telnet.exe. If you are not using

Who Are These People, Anyway?

Chapter 7

Windows 95, this same program can be found at many download sites on the Web. From the menu bar in the telnet program window, select **Connect/Remote System...** and enter the numerical telnet address. Press [Enter] and telnet will do the rest.

The first question you will be asked is "Use cool ansi screen?" Answer "N", for No, here. You will then be asked to create a name. Pick anything you like! Remember, this is a fantasy game, so the sky's the limit. If you want to be Galahad or Sir Gawain, be prepared to have to pick another character, as popular names will probably already be in use! However, you could always be Arthur's long lost nephew, Harold.

Next, you will be asked to verify this name. If it's spelled right, answer "Y", for yes. If it's not, answer "N", for No, to return to the name creation line. Now you'll be asked to supply a password. This is so no one can log on as you and play the game using your character. Choose a password and enter it here. You will be prompted to enter it again to verify.

Now it's time to create the character's general attributes. First, you must choose a race. The options will be spelled out for you. If you don't know what the attributes of each race are, type the word "help" after the prompt.

You'll be presented with a list of races and what strengths, weaknesses and alignment (a general code of ethics) each predominantly encompasses. Press [Enter] to leave the Help area, then type in your choice. I have chosen to be a Halfling for this example.

The next question asks if you want to be male or female. Since you're creating a character here, you don't have to reflect reality. So, decide which you prefer. It may be your chance to see how the other half lives! Now you will be asked to choose a profession for your character, known as a class. This is how your character primarily

Who Are These People, Anyway?

Chapter 7

spends his or her time. The choices you are given will correspond to the rules laid out for the races. I have chosen Paladin for my halfling's career, a class which has a lot of restrictions to it.

This is an advanced class. To find out what restrictions apply to each class, you can type "help paladin" at the prompt to get a detailed listing of the qualities of this class. If you were to choose mage, the command, of course, would be "Help Mage," etc. Since this class has a set alignment of "good," I am not offered a choice for that option. However, most character classes must decide if the they wish to be good, bad or chaotic.

The alignment one chooses affects how one acts in the MUD; failure to act according to your alignment can cause you to be dumped from the game. In a nutshell, good characters do what most folks would consider to be "good," bad characters are selfish and look out for themselves and chaotic (or neutral) characters are somewhere in the middle. For your first time out, you will probably want to be a chaotic character, for ease of play.

Here is what our screen looks like so far:

> By What Name Do You Wish To Be Known? Did I get that right, Maldoon? (Y/N)?
> New character.
> Give me a password for Maldoon:
> Please retype password:
> The Following Races are Available:
>   human elf dwarf giant gnome halfling orc birdman centaur drow
> What is your Race (help for more information)? What is your Sex (M/F)? Select a
> Class   [mage cleric thief warrior monk bard paladin]: Paladins have many rp
> restrictions to them.
> Read help Paladin to see Paladin rules.
>
> You are of good alignment.
> Press [Enter] to continue.

Who Are These People, Anyway?

Chapter 7

Now you need to enter your Email address. This is so if you lose your password, you will be able to get another one. This extra level of password security is to prevent anyone from jumping on as your character, then changing your password so you can't get on again. It's also to prevent anyone from pretending to be you and obtaining your password. Note that your password does not appear on the screen when you type it. You will need to keep it somewhere so you don't forget it, or there won't be a log of it!

Now comes the fun part of character building: customizing the character. Although you can skip this step, it is what makes your character part of your personality, and it gives it a life of its own.

Let's select "Y", for yes, at this prompt. A screen comes up that lists the skills and categories that are available for your character. Don't worry about the length of the list or forgetting something if it scrolls over your screen while you're working on this section. You can get it back at any time by typing:

```
LIST
```

Also listed will be how many "creation points" (or CPs) you currently have. This is the number of points you have to spend in building your character. You will note that it's probably not very high. That's because CPs are earned as you advance through the dungeon. Also, some skills are given to you by default. Look these over so you don't waste CPs on a skill you already possess.

Looking at the list, you will see that next to each skill is a number. This number is the amount of creation points you must spend to gain that skill. To add a skill, you type:

```
ADD
```

Who Are These People, Anyway?

Chapter 7

at the prompt under the chart, followed by the skill name as it appears on the chart. Let's add "detection" to this character we're creating. We only have 5 creation points, and detection is going to use all five, so this will be the only skill added at this time. Now we have added the group of skills known as "detection." When you've added as much as you can, type:

```
done
```

at the prompt.

Now come the rules. This screen will let you know exactly what you need to do in order to play the game correctly. Read these, learn them, maybe even print them.

There's no recourse if you break the rules and are dropped from the game. Remember, these are being run at educational and research facilities. They expect you to be literate and to pay attention. The screen that is displayed here is actually a pared down version, a message of the day. You will need to type:

```
rules
```

at the prompt to get a detailed instruction set. Let's finish the MOTD and then check out the rules.

Once the MOTD has run, we're put into the first area of the MUD, called Merc's Mud School. Characters under level five default here. A message will appear on the screen to warn you that the MUD you're in has player interaction and rules which allow one player's character to kill another.

Who Are These People, Anyway?

Chapter 7

```
Warning: This is a pkill mud. You are gonna die at some point on here.

The first thing you might want to type is HELP RULES or check out
Dragon's home page at http://jgsdos.brooktrout.com:8000/dragon


Entrance to Mud School
This is the entrance to the Merc Mud School. Go north to go through mud school.
If you have been here before and want to go directly to the arena, go south.

A sign warns "You may not pass these doors once you have passed level 5."
Num    Name Unread Description
===    ============ ====== ============
 1>    General  [ 76] General discussion
 2>    Announce [ 10] Announcements from Immortals
 3>    Bugs     [  4] Typos, bugs, errors, ideas
 4>    Personal [  0] Personal messages
 5>    Guild    [  0] Guild Notes

Your current board is General.
You can only read notes from this board.
There is no war declared at this time.
```

Since we haven't read the rules yet, this isn't going to make much sense. Typing "Help Rules" at this point explains what we're viewing here. Make sure you do so, before continuing. Note also that there is another warning that you will not be notified if you break any of the rules. You're on your own out here, which may seem cold, but the thrill of the online MUD is intoxicating enough that pretty soon the rules are second nature.

Who Are These People, Anyway?

Chapter 7

The MUD atmosphere

A few words about the atmosphere of the MUD: This form of online chat can be almost addicting. Before we head into the actual rules of play on this particular MUD, you may want to set some limits for yourself. It sounds funny to say that, but I have known people who joined MUDs and found them so fascinating that they did begin to neglect real life studies and duties to stay and play in them. This is a fascinating study in imagination, interaction and mind games, but it can also be somewhat escapist. Bear some rules in mind of your own, while embarking on the MUD journey.

This is not real life! This is a game! You will meet many people, many romantic faces, doing remarkable things. It's not real. Too many times people forget this, and let the images in their mind dictate their emotions. You can feel the emotions of love, anger, grief and all ranges in between, that's part of the fun. It's not fun when you let them take over and become your real emotions.

This is a different type of chat than we've been discussing. While the players are real people behind keyboards, the facades they put to screen are, by definition, not themselves or their true personalities. Make sure you take the time to learn the person behind the mask before agreeing to meet or in any way contact them outside of the game.

Also, be prepared to face the fact that a lot of these folks will not want contact outside of the game. Don't take it as a personal comment on yourself, just be aware that a lot of people take gaming very seriously, and there is almost an unwritten code that contact outside of the game is dishonorable. By suggesting they do so, you may insult them. It's best to not go into a MUD looking to make friends, but rather, to take friends you already know into the MUD with you to play.

Who Are These People, Anyway?

Chapter 7

Don't take events in the game too seriously. Your best friend may choose to be an evilly aligned character, which means that they will need to act according to that alignment. If they kill you, it's part of the game. Fortunately, it's not real, and you can always create another character. The point in these games is to have fun, as it is in any game.

MUD commands

There is a common lingo used on the MUD games. This dialect is the command set you can use to perform various activities while on the game. They are broken down into groups, designated by what types of objects are affected by them.

MOVEMENT	GROUP
north south east west up down exits recall sleep wake rest stand follow	group gtell split

OBJECTS	INFORMATION / COMMUNICATION
get put drop give sacrifice donate wear wield hold recite quaff zap brandish lock unlock open close pick bash inventory equipment look compare eat drink fill list buy sell value	help credits areas commands socials report score time weather where who channels config description password title auction chat music question answer shout yell emote pose say tell bug idea typo note wizlist slist spells autoexit autoloot autosac blank brief combine prompt

COMBAT	OTHER
kill flee kick rescue disarm backstab cast wimpy	! save quit pagelength practice train

149

Who Are These People, Anyway?

Chapter 7

Some other words you will see are words that define the kind of MUD you are playing. These come from the type of code (programming language) used to create the MUD, where the mythology and background of the MUD is based, what sense of humor the creators had, and other resources. Although each MUD will have some of it's own peculiarities in this regard, there is also a common set of words that you should know before embarking. By knowing this basic lingo, you can tell what kind of MUD you're entering before you log on, and so can make a more informed decision on whether this is the kind of MUD you'd enjoy playing. Most MUDs will have this information listed in a description somewhere, either on a web page they may have set up, or in the general information you can get in their MOTD.

Word	Definition
level	What advances you have achieved in the game
pkill	Player kill, meaning that you fight and kill other players as well as MUD denizens
theme	If applicable, what set of myths or fantasy works the story is based on
multi-play	If you are allowed to play more than one character at a time
bot	A character being run by a computer, forbidden in most MUDs
quest	A MUD with a goal, not just exploring and gaining experience
race	What basic phenotype your character is
class	Your character's profession
multi-classed	A character with more than one profession, not allowed on all MUDs
role-playing	Interacting with other characters as your character, not always required
equipment	Items your character uses within the MUD

Who Are These People, Anyway?

Chapter 7

Equipment for a MUD excursion

There are a few things that you will want on a MUD excursion that most newbies don't consider but are infinitely handy.

Graph paper

The first of these is graph paper. You'll find that you make a lot of twists and turns, and you'll be wanting to map your way through so you can get back out when you want to.

Pencil

Next, of course, is a pencil (not a pen) and a big eraser like you had in grade school. The reason you need these is that invariably, you will find that the map just isn't as accurate as you'd like it to be, so you need to be able to change it.

Light

Have a good strong light in the room. Text screens are sometimes hard to read.

Printer or a journal

A printer is handy for printing out directions and signs you may see along the way containing clues you need to remember. Some folks keep a journal, to add realism to the adventure and save important information. Blank books are good for this and are relatively inexpensive and easy to find at most book stores.

MUD tips

There are also a few tips for playing that are useful once you get into the MUD.

Who Are These People, Anyway?

Chapter 7

Always look in gates and doors before you pass through them

Ambushes, especially in pkill MUDs, can be costly. Remember, when your character is dead, they may be dead for good, which means you lose all those points. Even if you are resurrected, you've lost your equipment and usually a few levels.

Watch your back!

Always take all the items from a corpse when you kill a monster. The command GET ALL CORPSE will do this for you, and is a valuable way to gain treasure. Items you can't use at the moment may be handy later or you may be able to sell or trade them for items you need.

Don't cross people of a higher level than yourself

In a pkill MUD, you can lose your character this way. Read every sign you come to. Check for secret exits before settling for the obvious ones listed with EXITS. Always use the CONSIDER command before entering into a battle. Knowing what you're up against is highly valuable.

Choosing a MUD

Now that we have the glossary and the tips, let's look at the description of another MUD and determine if it's one in which you're interested. You can play in more than one MUD at a time; it's not necessary to finish one quest before beginning another.

Check out a few MUDs and see which you like the best. They are all different levels of skills, programming expertise and themes. The best way to MUD is probably to do several at once, getting experience and knowledge in one you can carry to the next.

Who Are These People, Anyway?

Chapter 7

A very good way to find MUDs is through the World Wide Web. Point your browser to http://www.mudconnect.com, which is a wonderfully designed site with access to over 400 MUDs, including their descriptions and links to their home pages, system administrator's Email and Telnet addresses.

Let's take an example to decipher the description of a MUD. We're looking for a MUD based on Roger Zelazny's "Chronicles of Amber." We'd like it to not be a player kill dungeon, and we'd like to be able to use extended character classes and races, instead of a basic set. Let's look at Blue Facial MUD first:

> Blue Facial MUD
> Last Updated: January 11, 1997
> Code Base: Merc
> Site: dallet.channel1.com 1234 [205.240.163.3]
> Admin Email: mudoper@dallet.channel1.com
> Theme: Medieval sword and sor. Rolplaying.
> Check Connection
> Connect to Blue Facial MUD
> Blue Facial MUD Statistics
>
> •Multi-Play: No •Player-Kill: Yes •Extended Race Selection•Extended Class Selection•Multi-classing Allowed•Equipment Saved•Quests Available•Character Approval Unnecessary•Roleplaying Is Required

Armed with the glossary, we can see that Blue Facial does not fit our needs at all! Although it allows extended races and characters, it's a player kill dungeon. This is also going to be an advanced MUD, as is evidenced by the fact that roleplaying is required, and you battle other player characters as well as the programmed hostile MUD creatures found in most MUDs.

Now let's look at Dreamshadow, the Legacy of The Three:

Who Are These People, Anyway?

Chapter 7

> Dreamshadow: The Legacy of Three
> Code Base: Lp
> Site: telmaron.com 3333 [204.180.173.1]
> Admin Email: dreamer@telmaron.com
> Theme: Varied
> Check Connection
> Connect to Dreamshadow: The Legacy of Three
> Dreamshadow: The Legacy of Three Homepage
> Dreamshadow: The Legacy of Three Statistics
>
> •Multi-Play: Limited •Player-Kill: Restricted •Extended Race Selection•Extended Class Selection•Multi classing Allowed•Equipment Saved•Quests Available•Character Approval Unnecessary

Now this one is much better suited! We may have to give up our idea of walking the Pattern on a MUD (since this MUD isn't directly related to Zalazny's *Chronicles*), but this one will certainly come a lot closer than the other to what we're looking for. While you may have a specific idea of what you want in a MUD, some prioritizing of these details may be needed to find a suitable game. Taking a little time and finding just the right MUDs for you can make this experience a lot more rewarding.

So now you're in the MUD, how do you interact with the other players? Well, that depends on the type of MUD you've chosen and what the rules are there. Some MUDs don't require role-playing or interaction of any sort, although that would defeat the purpose of gaming online as a way to meet people. Some require interaction only with computer generated characters, which again isn't a very good way to meet people. So let's go with the assumption that you want to meet people and that's why you're here. Looking over the list of commands, you'll note some of them are related to types of vocal communication. To speak to another character, all you need to do is to choose one of these forms of vocal communication and

Who Are These People, Anyway?

Chapter 7

use it. For instance, you can chant, sing or say something to a character simply by choosing that command, then typing it into the buffer along with the message you wish to pass on:

```
say Help! Where am I?
*You say Help! Where am I?*
```

One final note regarding gaming in MUDs. Unlike poker or blackjack or some other games that you can find online to play with other folks, MUDs are primarily strategy and mind games, with very little luck involved. Don't get too frustrated when things aren't handed to you as they are needed. That's the point of these games, to find it yourself and complete the quest yourself using your wits and what alliances you can make. If you give up the first time out, you will probably miss what the fuss is all about. Take time to go through the merc school, if it's offered, to gain some skills and to gain some accomplishments. A little encouragement goes a long way, and in a MUD, practice makes perfect.

Safe forums

Another reason you'll find people online is the fact that online forums and chat rooms are safe forums. Here is a place where you can pretty much hold any opinion you wish, with little fear of repercussion. This is also a forum where you can debate these opinions for hours with all sorts of interesting people. "But you can do that in real life too," you might be thinking. Some people can't, and you'll find a lot of those folks online. The reasons they can't are as varied as the people themselves.

Some folks online suffer from a disorder called "agoraphobia." It's an abnormal fear of being helpless in an embarrassing or inescapable situation. It's characterized especially by avoiding open or public

Who Are These People, Anyway?

Chapter 7

places. This disorder can leave someone virtually housebound and without contact. Online interaction is a safe way for these folks to get out and explore and talk to others. Without the risk of being in an inescapable situation (you can always turn the computer off) these people can find whole worlds they never knew existed out on the net.

Other people find the anonymity offered by online chat to be a great enticement to release themselves from self-censoring behavior. While this is generally freeing, it's important to remember that the people onscreen are humans and not release yourself to the point of being rude and unacceptable. But for those folks who are very shy, online anonymity can help them open up. Again, it's the lack of repercussion that makes this possible, the fact that you can hold an idea and not face any real harm if you express it. With enough practice in the cyberworld, I've seen people who didn't relate very well in person come out of their shells and be far less withdrawn. Success breeds success, and it's true with communication skills as well.

Speaking of communication skills, that's another thing that can be developed by practicing online. Without the physical clues we use to determine mood, action, intent and thought behind words, we have to become more adept at using the words in the language more effectively.

In addition, you learn how much you rely on those visual and audio clues once they've been removed. You learn how to choose exactly the right word to fit your tone and intent, and you can also learn the value of an apology when a joke offends or a comment doesn't get to the person the way you intended it to get there.

You can also learn the value of a small thing, like a smiley face properly applied. With enough practice, you can tell when someone's genuinely trying to talk with you and work with you,

Who Are These People, Anyway?

Chapter 7

and when that smiley face is actually a tight lipped grimace. If you're very perceptive, you can take what doesn't work and discard it, take what works and use it more, and end up a much better communicator than when you started!

Because these forums are safe, you will find a much more eclectic selection of them online than you will in your typical neighborhood. Also, while these types of groups may exist in your neighborhood, more unpopular or less politically correct ones may be difficult to locate. Not so online! This is another reason people chat online, because of the immense variety and ease of getting information.

This is a place where you can finally break the infamous rule of not talking about politics or religion. When I was growing up, that's how I was taught: if one wants to communicate with someone, never talk about politics or religion. Now that's all changed, there are rooms and channels especially for that purpose! If you've never debated the merits of Christianity versus Buddhism with anyone but other Christians, your view is going to be severely limited. Now, with online forums, you can find out what the Buddhists are saying. You may even find they're not all that different from Christians in a lot of respects.

I once saw a chat with a group of people who heavily supported the National Rifle Association. A group of antigun activists was also in the room. They were talking quite intelligently about the pros and cons of gun ownership. Did anyone radically change their opinion and join the NRA or sell all their rifles? I doubt it. But what did happen is a group of people got to talk to another group of people, safely and peacefully, and find out what that other group was saying. This is the kind of situation that in real life has the potential for violence and all kinds of upset. Online, reduced to text and words, without the bias of not liking someone's hair length or goatee, it became an intelligent, mostly reasonable discussion.

Who Are These People, Anyway?

Chapter 7

Resources

Another reason people chat online is to find new and interesting web sites to surf. People who collect interesting URLs and sounds have whole channels devoted to their trade. There are also rooms and channels devoted to the trade of the ascii art macros we discussed earlier.

If you like to cruise the web, and are interested in some of the more bizarre offerings it has, you might like to check out these channels. If you're using mIRC 5.x, you can actually set it to pickup URLs automatically out of the chat room. Click on the menu on the toolbar labeled "File" then choose "Options." Click on the tab marked "URL Catcher." This brings up the URL catcher options to allow mIRC to pick up URLs from the channel's interactive screens. It will retrieve an URL automatically from a channel, /query message or even DCC chat.

Click on the option marked "Enable URL catcher." Next, place checks next to Activate Browser Window. In the long box at the bottom, place the location of your web browser. Now, when you're in a room, the URL catcher will automatically record all URLs as they are sent to screen.

To visit a URL, simply click on the icon that reads "URL." You can tell if there's a new URL by the border of this box, which will be red when a new URL is added. To view an URL, highlight it with your left mouse button.

Now with your right mouse button, click on the highlighted URL and choose "View." MIRC will open your web browser and display the chosen URL. You can set the URL catcher to delete new URLs after opening in the original options screen if you so desire.

Who Are These People, Anyway?

Chapter 7

What constitutes an interesting URL? That's up the viewer! I'm going to list a few here for you, so you can see what kinds of things people are looking for. Remember, URLs change, sometimes daily, but as of this writing, these are current. Who knows, by using this as a jumping off place, you can find all kinds of kooky, goofy or downright strange places all by yourself with little work.

Examples of some interesting URLS
http://www.nwdc.com/~demona/soul.htm   Sell Your Soul... Online
http://www.netcreations.com/magicurl/index.html   Random Web Sites
http://sunsite.unc.edu/personality/keirsey.html   Personality Assessment
http://curry.edschool.Virginia.EDU/go/frog/   Frog Dissection
http://www.ftech.net/~madsite/   Mad Scientists
http://www.ebay.com/aw/   Auction (for real junk)
http://www.rockhall.com/   Rock N Roll Hall Of Fame
http://www.netmind.com/e-minder/e-minder.html   E-Mail Reminders
http://www.ozchannel.com/vegemite/vegemite.html   Vegemite
http://www.godiva.com/index.html   Godiva
http://sunsite.unc.edu/louvre/net/   Louvre
http://www.ari.net/se/   Music you might like

Who Are These People, Anyway?

Chapter 7

Examples of some interesting URLS (Continued)
http://www.teleport.com/~dkossy/ Kooks Museum
http://www.cs.cornell.edu/Info/People/ckline/humor/maillist.html Mother of all Humor
http://www.primenet.com/~ken_h/bradpage.htm Brad Page
http://www.lyrics.ch/ Lyrics to almost everything

As I said, some people also collect interesting sounds, called "wavs." To find these, scour around the web for download libraries and FTP sites offering these sound clips from movies, radio shows, songs and television shows.

A well placed wav can say loads that a hundred words would never have conveyed. In most cases, you can tell by the name of the clip what it plays. Some people like to use the sound command with sounds that don't really exist, so make sure you ask "Is that a real wav?" before requesting it.

Also, remember, this is a trading situation. If you want to get some new wavs, go in with some, and see if you can reciprocate. That's what keeps those kinds of channels alive and operating! The same goes with the other trading rooms. The more you can share with the others, the better the room or channel ultimately is, so keep those eyes and ears open for things to share with others.

Some people come online to get involved in joke and email circles. There are also rooms and channels with good addresses to get onto these kinds of listservs. A listserv is a program that allows web servers and network servers to send to large amount of people at a time, instead of just 100 or 200.

Who Are These People, Anyway?

Chapter 7

You would be amazed at how many of these there are. There's everything form servers that will send you a new word every day for vocabulary building to ones that send out a weekly synopsis of strange events from newspapers throughout the world.

I used to belong to something called a "round robin" email, which is email sent out to a few people who reply to all the parties on the email with their responses, like a meeting without the conference room. We had a limerick round robin that went for several months, where one person would make a subject and we all had a turn at creating a limerick about it. Some round robins can be very large. I know of a screenwriter's listserv that is usually over 700K of text file! This is a mobile message board, which travels the web instead of having any particular home on a site or service.

Red light district

There are some channels and rooms you probably want to avoid. Some of them have names that if you're not in the know, you won't realize that you don't want to be there.

Warez rooms

Primary among these are rooms or channels advertising themselves as "warez" rooms. This is another word for pirated software, which is what it's called when you get a piece of software illegally. People in these rooms are trading in licensed software products, selling them at a reduced cost. It's important to know why this is wrong, to better understand why you don't want to do it (besides the fact that it's illegal).

When you purchase a software package, you don't actually purchase the software contained on the disks. Rather, you purchase the right to use that software on as many computers are specified on the license. This is how the software developers make their money,

Who Are These People, Anyway?

Chapter 7

through the sale of the licenses. If you accept pirated software, you're stealing not only from the company that produces the software package, but also from the person(s) who developed the program.

Phreaking

Phreaking is stealing someone's credit card number. Obviously, this is an unlawful pursuit and something you want to avoid. Unfortunately, there are people out there trading stolen credit card numbers. I assure you, you want to have no part of this! The law looks down very much on this kind of activity.

Why will you see it so prominently displayed on IRC servers? Because generally speaking, the Internet is not a regulated body, being international in scope. It's hard to apply the rules of one country onto the citizens of another, and it's generally difficult to tell what country you may have hopped into. That means it's up to you to know the terms that are associated with illegal activities, and stay away from them!

Pornography

A fair amount of pornography is traded on the Internet as well. Before going further here, let me throw out a definition for you. According to Merriam Webster, pornography is the depiction of erotic behavior (as in pictures or writing) intended only to cause sexual excitement.

The key part of this definition are the words "intended only." A nude picture is not necessarily a pornographic one. Even a nude picture of an individual or individuals engaged in sexual activity may not be a pornographic picture. The decision of whether a photograph is pornographic is very much a factor of the viewer as opposed to any outside "rules."

Who Are These People, Anyway?

Chapter 7

There are rooms and channels where nudes are being traded, and some of these are indeed pornographic to most people. These channels and rooms aren't hidden, they are usually very easy to spot. Again, although the laws in the US about what constitutes pornography may be what you're familiar with, the laws about what constitutes pornography in Sweden where your IRC server is located may not be the same, so there's no reason to go to any effort to hide these types of channels. If you go to a channel called "XXX Men," expect to receive photographs of men engaged in sexual activity.

At no time do you want to enter any room advertising itself as "child," "teen" or "underage" picture trading. This is illegal in the United States and can result in jail terms for a considerable length of time. There are ways to find out who's downloading these types of pictures and you don't want that trail to lead to your door. Erasing your hard drive is not enough to get rid of this data, either. There are ways to read files that have been deleted, secure deleted and even formatted off a drive. Do yourself a favor: don't even go.

If you are of age and choose to enter adult trading rooms or channels, these files will be sent to you via DCC. To be safe, you should download to a floppy disk and run a virus scan over any file you receive to be sure you aren't downloading a virus.

Trojan horses (files that piggyback onto or disguise themselves as another file) aren't viruses because they don't replicate within your machine. Rather, these files usually drop a huge bomb on your system in the form of a batch file that runs the next time you boot up.

I have seen these kinds of simple files format your hard drive while you sit helpless to stop it. I've also seen more intricate ones that will send your password and screen name to a thief on another computer. As soon as they have your password, they have the key

Who Are These People, Anyway?

Chapter 7

to your account. There are even files of this type that can cause physical harm to your computer by causing the hard drive to return to the same position over and over, ruining it.

You can't get a virus by reading an email message, it's a file that must be downloaded. Just practice safe netting, and you'll be fine.

Romance

Another reason people come online is to find romance. There are plenty of rooms and channels on which to meet a member of the gender to which you're attracted for amorous meetings.

These rooms and channels have many abbreviations that may not seem obvious to you. By using these, the /list on an IRC becomes a great personal ad. Have you ever checked out the classified ads for homes in a newspaper? You'll see 1 bdrm 2.5 bth on wdd lot... what kind of meaning does that have? To someone who's hunting for a home, that's a two bedroom house with two bathrooms with bathtubs and one without, on a wooded lot.

The same kind of code is on the romance channels you'll find online. "F" is female. "M" is male. "F4M" is a female looking for a male. "BBW" is "big beautiful woman"—this is the Rubenesque set. "S" is single, "W" is white, "E" or "Ebony" is used more often than black. "TV" is probably not a room to discuss television, it usually means transvestite. "CD" isn't music, it's cross dressing. "TS" is transsexual.

Usually you'll find these rooms labeled "TSTV," rarely will there be one alone. "Cur" is curious. Rooms and channels will have this code as a name, usually several of them in a row, with no spaces. So "TSTV4CurF" is a channel devoted to transsexual transvestites looking for curious females.

Who Are These People, Anyway?

Chapter 7

There are room and channels more straight forward, however. Some advertise "Looking for Love," some are "Looking for Mr. Right." There are "Cheating On Spouse" rooms, "Wife Home Alone" channels and "Spankings here." These room titles leave little to the imagination, but they are honest about what's hanging around cyberspace in them. There are also "Happily Married" and "I found Love Online" channels, so don't get too depressed at your prospects! I've heard more than one successful online love story so I know it happens.

Support

Some people chat online to fill a void in their lives. They may be in a new home, in a new town, going to school for the first time, or suffering a loss, such as a divorce or a death of a spouse. They may be insomniacs with no one to speak to at the hour of night they're on, or they may work an odd shift at work and find themselves up at all different hours. There are channels online for nurses, police officers and emergency workers as well as romance and interest channels.

Occupations such as these are generally at odd hours and all hours, and these rooms are great not only because they're populated by people working the same hours as you, but also because these people share the same kind of stresses you have. It's like an international break room where folks can relax and get over the cares of the work day, no matter when that day may begin and end.

There are also channels for survivors of abuse and also for alcoholics anonymous. These are the types of things that sometimes you don't really feel like waiting for a support group to meet every other Tuesday when you're hurting and looking for a friendly ear. Online is a good place for this, since it's anonymity can afford some folks freedom to speak they might otherwise not feel they had.

Who Are These People, Anyway?

Chapter 7

Like the occupational rooms and channels I mentioned above, here are people who understand what you're feeling. They've been through it and they can empathize with you. Remember, these aren't going to be the same as going to a licensed professional and getting real treatment. They can be a wonderful, safe support group, with folks who listen and care. You have the opportunity to help others in these kinds of rooms as well by being supportive.

If you feel like a story is too outlandish, you need to remember, everyone's reality is subjective. The person may be making the whole thing up, in which case, they need attention for whatever reason. Look at these people as people who need help and support too, and never call someone a liar in these types of channels! You aren't there, and the most fantastic story may be true.

Conclusion

Looking back over this chapter, we can see that there are a lot of reasons why people chat. Some folks are looking for a little company to play games with, some are looking to engage in fantastic adventures with folks who share the same kind of daydreams as they do. There are people looking for a safe forum in which to discuss any kind of subject. Then you have your romance seekers, your lonely people and your odd-hours people. There's even people just looking for an ear and a shoulder at 0400 and online is a great place to find it.

Basically, the point of this section is that people online are just people. They're online to communicate because that's what we, as humans, do. By choosing to use channels and rooms that reflect your interests, you'll find an amazing variety of people that, while

Who Are These People, Anyway?

Chapter 7

in different countries, with different jobs and lives than your own, nonetheless share some commonality that makes the differences between people seem very small.

It doesn't matter if you're tall, short, black, white, gay, bisexual, heterosexual, fat, thin, lonely, or happily married, somewhere out there, there's someone who shares the same interests and fears as you. This is why people chat online, to get to learn how the other half lives and in so doing, learn how to better themselves and their own lives, and maybe have some fun in the process.

Nothing like a rousing evening in the dungeon to make a fairly dull desk job take on new life! By taking advantage of this easy-to-reach medium, you can add a lot of spice with very little effort to your life. That's the final reason people chat online, to add to an already full life something that can only come from interaction with a different culture. Online is a safe place to do so.

Safety On The Net

8

The Good Guys 172
AOL's ordained structure of volunteers 172
Guides 173
Rangers 173
People Connection Hosts 173
Kids Only (KO) hosts 174
The Bad Guys 177
Phishers 180
Carding 186
Warez 187
Wormers 189
Cyberpunks 190
Phreakers 192
Whacker 193
Wannabe 195
Online stalkers 195
Physical Security 198
Passwords and physical security measures 198
Safety in meeting people from online 200

Now that I've told you about the great people you meet online and how safe it is, let's talk about the seamier side of the cyber world. Just as every city has its bad part of town where folks would rather not go after the sun sets, the cyber world also has its less than savory people and areas.

Also, as in real life, you can take precautions to make sure you don't run into these folks who mean you harm in the cyber city. It's actually much easier to protect yourself online than it is in the real world, where thieves can snatch your bag while you're just passing by. In the cyber world, you almost have to give it to them.

Therefore, I'm going to explain typical scams, how to recognize them, how to avoid them and how to do other normal activities safely so you don't inadvertently hand your valuable information over to a would-be thief.

Safety On The Net

Chapter 8

We'll also learn what information online thieves find valuable so you know what to protect. Passwords and credit card numbers are obvious but a thief can also do a lot of damage with your telephone and social security numbers!

We'll look at their language and their methods so you can be aware of what's going on around you. I'm not going to pretend to be able to get into the heads of people who do this kind of thing so I can't explain the motivations for this activity. Instead, I'll concentrate on what I know, which is how to keep from being suckered in and what to do if you are.

The Good Guys

As you travel the web and chat rooms, you're going to find two groups of people stand out amongst the crowds. One of these groups is helpful, friendly and working to help you. The members spend their time online teaching folks how to better use the system, their computers and other aspects of the online world. Then there's the other group, the people who are out to make your time online unpleasant and unnerving. I wish I could say that they weren't out there, but they are. Fortunately, the first group more than makes up for them, so let's look at them first.

AOL's ordained structure of volunteers

AOL has a distinct advantage over most proprietary online services: an officially ordained structure of volunteers helping people. These volunteers receive their accounts for free as a recognition of the value of the services they provide in volunteering for America Online. They choose to try to make the online community on that particular service more enjoyable for those users who are newer to the net.

Safety On The Net

Chapter 8

Guides

AOL has several groups of volunteers to assist you. They include *Guides*, who are by far the easiest to find. To locate a Guide on AOL, simply go to a room called "AOL Help," "AOL PC Help," "AOL Mac Help" or "AOL Windows Help." These areas are staffed in shifts by Guides who are there to help you learn to use AOL and your computer better. You will also find Guides roaming the chat rooms and forum areas to answer questions for members.

Rangers

Another AOL volunteer group is the Rangers. These folks, with the prefix "Rnger," are found primary in the Discover forum (a default conference room for new AOL members) and the chat areas called "Tips and Tricks." Rangers also hold classes for new folks on how to use AOL's many features and areas. These people are also skilled in chat room hosting and can show you how to use chat skills to the best advantage.

People Connection Hosts

The People Connection Hosts are a third group. These people, while more numerous than either of the other two groups, are somewhat harder to find because they don't have a standardized name tag. Most of these you will find are called "HOST ___" or "Host ___." The blank will be filled by whatever name the host selects.

Some are called "Host RDI" (for Red Dragon Inn, a free-form role playing area), some are called "TS" (ThirtySomething, a channel for 30-40 year olds), while others are "TMP" (The Meeting Place, a gathering area for folks who are looking to meet someone offline as well as online).

173

Safety On The Net

Chapter 8

You can generally identify a host on the system because they do not leave the chat area. Instead, they stay and greet participants, run topics and generally make the atmosphere nicer. Some of them run games (mostly trivia) in rooms called "Game Parlors." Some of them read fortunes in forums, others are chat leaders who host themed chats on a regular basis in various rooms.

You can usually find a listing of these themed chats in a FAQ (Frequently Asked Questions file) at the forum's main screen. This will tell what chats are held, the schedule and any guests who are slated to appear. AOL isn't the only place to have themed chats with guests! You can find these on the web, Prodigy, CompuServe and other proprietary services, although not with the regularity of America Online's.

Kids Only (KO) hosts

A fourth group of AOL volunteer chat hosts resides in the Kids Only area, called "KO." This group has the standardized tag "KO," and you will find them only in the AOL Kids Only rooms. The KOs make sure kids online have a good working knowledge of basic online safety conventions, and ensure that older kids don't come to the area to disrupt it.

Something very important to remember about the KOs' ability to safeguard your children, however, is that they're only able to tell your children how to report people who are bothering them. They can't see your child's screen and have no way of knowing if your child is being harassed by someone.

The other kids' areas on AOL also have chat hosts who are trained to work specifically with kids. You will find these people in the non-AOL specific kids' areas, such as Cartoon Network and Nickelodeon. More of these areas won't allow children into them if a chat host is not available to supervise the area, so you can feel

Safety On The Net

Chapter 8

more assured that there will be someone available to help your children if they need it. These caring individuals represent the top of the heap of what you'll find online, so when you're exploring this service, avail yourself of them!

You will find people on IRCs and web-based chats performing the same duties and not even getting free online access for it. Almost any night of the week you can find channels called "IRC Help," "MIRC Help," "IRC Newbies" and so on. People in these channels will help you learn how to better enjoy your IRC experience.

I have found these types of people to a lesser extent on the visual mediums, too. Some of these people have identifying comments in their ULS listing, like "Help you set up your camera" or "Helping test Videophone." Fortunately, these people are not difficult to find, no matter what the medium.

If you're using a service that doesn't provide a volunteer staff, there are still plenty of places to get help using the system and reporting issues you have. One is their customer service, whose number is usually listed on the software's manual or packaging. Another choice is to write to the postmaster or webmaster at the service's main Email. This looks like "postmaster@msn.com", for instance.

Also, never forget, help is easily available by clicking on the word "HELP" at the top of your screen! These help files are usually interactive, and all you have to do is select your issue to be taken through the more common solutions.

If you're having system trouble, a Help menu for Windows 95 is located on the menu that opens when you click the [Start] button. This is particularly helpful if you're having trouble getting your modem recognized by any software you may be using. Windows 95 will walk you step by step through a diagnostic to ensure the issue is simply the modem not setting up correctly and not faulty hardware. By learning how to use these, you will endear yourself

175

Safety On The Net

Chapter 8

to countless technical support people who are used to calls from people who could have answered the question for themselves by opening the manual!

If you can't find the answer anywhere, and you've looked, next try asking someone in the room. Usually, people are more than willing to help a person who's learning. It may be that your question's answer involves a trick that's not common knowledge. People love to share these shortcuts. People are a good resource for you, and asking questions is a way to meet folks and get started in conversations if you do it right.

Don't come into a channel and start yelling "Does anyone know how to fix this?" in all uppercase letters over someone's theological discussion on the several levels of Hell portrayed in Dante's Inferno and what they mean to modern Buddhism. Pick a more appropriate segue and you'll have much better results. Maybe this would work: "Dante was probably trying to make colored chat on mIRC 5.1 when he wrote that."

> *Don't come into a channel and start yelling "Does anyone know how to fix this?" in all uppercase letters...pick a more appropriate segue. Remember, people are talking and interrupting them is rude.*

Whatever you choose, remember that people are talking, and interrupting them is rude and won't make you any friends. If it seems to be a casual conversation about how many string jokes one person knows, this might be easier to introduce your topic into.

These people we've been discussing can be very helpful. They give generously of their time and expertise to help you and I become more comfortable and productive in online communities. But what about the other group I mentioned earlier? How do you manage to avoid running into the bad guys, and what does one do when you

Safety On The Net

Chapter 8

have? You need to know how to keep yourself safe and un-bothered while online, just as much as you need to know how to talk to people without being a pest. The folks we're looking at here aren't going to be your average person who's just sort of clueless. Rather, these people are coming online specifically to harass folks.

We'll look at some of the reasons why they are bad and how to keep yourself safe from them. As fast as technology advances, these people can circumvent the methods of blocking them. However, the techniques I'm going to give you work no matter what the technology does. In other words, although AOL, MSN and others are working to keep these folks away from you, they still find ways of getting to you, so you need to know good, common sense methods of fighting back.

Remember when you were a kid and you didn't feel well, your mother would bring you chicken soup, despite medical breakthroughs and medicinal changes. That's because no matter how fancy aspirin gets, chicken soup still does the job, and easily. Consider this to be the chicken soup of online safety measures. It won't cure the problem, but that's not something you can do. What you can do is keep your own little corner free of these pests.

The Bad Guys

They call themselves by many different names and think they're accomplishing great feats. However, when you strip off the name, you find the same thing underneath: a pest. These folks think they're demonstrating their intelligence and/or skill by cracking holes in online security, bothering people online, bothering people in Email, sending malicious files and just about anything else you can imagine to make your stay online as unpleasant as possible.

Safety On The Net

Chapter 8

Why? Mostly because they're either powerless in real life, in a real-life situation they find threatening or are just plain poorly socialized and don't care who they hurt as long as they have fun. I want to stress, these people are a tiny minority of the people online, but unfortunately, they are out there and they seem to have nothing better to do with their time. However, there are simple ways to thwart them. With a little patience, you can usually put these people off easily.

The first trick to battling these individuals is to know what they're trying to get from their behavior, then deny them that. No one does anything unless they're getting some kind of reward out of it.

> *I want to stress, these people are a tiny minority of the people online but, unfortunately, they are out there and they seem to have nothing better to do with their time. However, there are simple ways to thwart them.*

For instance, I may be writing this book because I enjoy the sound of my own typing, so as long as it keeps up, I'll keep writing! If I were to get a keyboard that made no noise, writing might not fulfill me.

Think about why you do the things you do. You go to work because you get paid. You may work overtime because it makes you feel valuable, or because it pays more or because occupies your otherwise vacant time. In each case, you get something for your effort, whether tangible or not.

Look at something besides work now. Why do you perform maintenance on your home? The cost of repair is usually more than the cost of preventative measures, not to mention the cost of replacing destroyed items, if your plumbing bursts for example.

How about your hobbies? They relax you, obviously, but you probably also get a sense of self worth by completing a project well. You prove to yourself you can do what ever it is, you feel creative, strong and worthwhile. If your hobby stops being worthwhile to

Safety On The Net

Chapter 8

you in this respect, most likely you will stop doing it. It's this mindset we're looking at when you're talking about an online pest. Most likely, the pest isn't being paid to be there bothering you! Neither is this something he does to keep his computer in working order and prevent costly repairs. What we have left is self esteem building.

So, in a nutshell, to get rid of a hardcore pest who's come online with no other purpose than to disrupt, you handle them just like you do someone who's acting inappropriately because they don't know better.

In Chapter 7 we discussed ignoring people who were bothering you. We're going to do the same thing here, only in a larger degree and somewhat modified depending on the activity involved. At the heart of it, we're going to stop paying them to do that to you and make them move on to someone who's more fun to bother, because they respond like the pest wants them to. Some of these other techniques will prevent them from doing you more harm than simply annoying you.

Let's look at some definitions first. These folks call themselves by different labels, depending on what particular annoying thing they enjoy doing the most.

Some of them are:

Safety On The Net

Chapter 8

Label	Activity
phishers	People who try to steal passwords.
carders	People who steal credit card numbers—they often have merchandise sent to a false address, then resell it at a profit.
pirates	Trade in commercial software, selling the program at a reduced price without granting the license.
warez	Same as pirating; avoid warez rooms and channels—this is illegal.
hackers	Break into company secured areas for the purpose of demonstrating weakness (NOTE: These people are actually helpful; their goal is to enhance security and they never do damage to the systems into which they break!).
whackers	Break into company secured areas for the purpose of doing damage.
crackers	Use simple editing programs to change aspects of a software package.
wannabes	Use windows based programs created by whackers to disrupt. They have no ability to whack on their own, however.
cyberpunk	Someone who is following in the footsteps of the characters created by writer William Gibson and is living out a heroic fantasy online.
wormer	Someone who writes virus programs designed to irretrievably corrupt data. Some programs may still run on a computer infected with a worm but saving data produced on them is generally worthless.
phreakers	People who cheat long-distance companies out of toll charges by using equipment designed to work around the company's toll system.

Let's look at these guys in depth.

Phishers

You will normally find *phishers* only on the proprietary services because they're after the password to your account. Generally, an ISP account isn't worth very much to a phisher. An account on a

Safety On The Net

Chapter 8

proprietary service, however, gives them opportunities. With this kind of account, a phisher can disturb folks who have limited ways of stopping the disruption, as opposed to going to an IRC server where the members can kick and ban the offending user. Below are some examples of the kind of messages phishers will send. Phishers work by sending an Instant Message or private message, called a "surf," to the unsuspecting user, using an official tone or meaningless technobabble.

The following examples were taken from AOL.

| Sector4G2C: | Sector 4G2C of our data base has lost all I/O functions. When the OH account logged onto our system, we were temporarily able to verify it as a registered user. Approximately 43 seconds ago, your verification was made void by loss of data in the Sector 4G3E. Now, due to AOL verification protocol, it is mandatory for us to re-verify your account. Please click "Respond" and re-state your password. Failure to comply will result in immediate account deletion. |

Note the sending name on this is "official sounding" and reflects the body of the message. You will also find this kind of surf being sent from names such as "BillingRep" and other names which at first glance might seem legitimate. The faux tech-talk also sounds official and is purposely confusing. For most users, the only clear parts of the message are the password request and the threat. The example below contains an even scarier threat to the recipient:

Safety On The Net

Chapter 8

> Urgent!!As your America Online account was in <<room name>>, it was the 17th account out of 22 members to be HACKED. This is **VITAL** that you comply with your America Online password, so that we may start trace. If you do not comply, you may be sentenced up to 75 years imprisonment, and may be fined up to 850,000 dollars due to the damages that the hacker has just accomplished on your account. Also if you do not comply your account will be TERMINATED due to America Online security reasons. Thank You. -AOL

The following surf uses the name of a prominent AOL board member in an attempt to coax the member into submitting his/her password:

> likewomen2: Hi, I am Steve Case (Founder of AOL) and I need you to reply back with your password in order to verify that you are a true AOL user and not a Hacker. Thank you for your cooperation.

It's unlikely, however, that AOL's founder would use such a tacky, unprofessional screen name, and he would never ask for your password (besides the security issues, I'm sure the founder of such a successful organization might have more important things to do than verify individual memberships).

Below is a surf sent to members in a new area, attempting to portray sending a password as a final step of registering the AOL account:

> DoWownsGKx Hello, I am a representative of the Division of WAOL(DoW) Corp. Due to a computer error, we are unable complete your membership to America Online. In order to correct this problem, we ask that you hit the 'Respond' key, and reply with your full name and password, so that the proper changes can be made to avoid cancellation of your account. Thank you for your time and cooperation. :-)

The following is an example of carding:

Safety On The Net

Chapter 8

> CLuMsY III: Dear User, due to a recent system crash our Credit Card database has been lost. Please respond to this with your Credit Card number within 2 minutes to restore the database.

Note that the following surf is asking not for passwords, but for a home telephone number. The surfer in this instance will probably telephone the user in an attempt to solicit credit card numbers, making this an indirect example of carding too:

> VVIIIIIVV: Good Evening AOL Member, Today was another day of our monthly system upgrade periods! We had a few errors in doing so. We jammed some of our memory chips to find that several members accounts info. was lost! We need you to reply with your correct billing information! Billing method, Zip Code, Phone Number and Address where you can be reached! We are so very sorry for this incovenience. Your account will be credited 35 free hours for your trouble! :-)

Some phishers use password sniffing programs to get passwords. These small programs, downloaded by the victim, record the first 25 or so keystrokes, save them to a file and send them via Email to an address where the phisher can decode them.

These programs have several characteristics that are common to this type of file. One is that they have the extension "exe" on them as they are executable files.

> To digress slightly: files come in several different types, which are distinguished by the letters after the dot in the file's name. For instance, **FILE.EXE** is a file that runs a program. **FILE.GIF** is a picture file in the **GIF** format. **FILE.AVI** is a file that will play a little movie on your computer using Window's Media Player.

183

Safety On The Net

Chapter 8

As you can tell in the examples I'm including (which are from real Email), all these files are programs despite what they claim to be.

The first file claims to be an auto-ignore utility, giving the user the ability to ignore instant messages from a specific party:

> Subj: Fwd: *****Auto - IGNORE*****
> Date: 97-06-03 18:02:47 EDT
> From: PestUser
> To: YourName
>
> File: SETUP.EXE (45086 bytes)
> DL Time (28800 bps): < 1 minute

The next file claims to be a movie file, for viewing on your computer. However, note that the file type is EXE, not AVI:

> Subj: Fwd: Hey Baby...
> Date: 97-06-03 18:03:58 EDT
> From: PestUser
> To: YourName
>
> File: MOVIE.EXE (316144 bytes)
> DL Time (28800 bps): < 3 minutes

Here's one claiming to be a password protection utility:

> Subj: Fwd: AOL Password Protection (URGENT)
> Date: 97-06-03 18:04:38 EDT
> From: PestUser
> To: YourName
>
> File: PW_FIX.EXE (26637 bytes)
> DL Time (28800 bps): < 1 minute

Safety On The Net

Chapter 8

The following password sniffer file claims to be several pornographic pictures sent together in one file. Note that it, too, is an EXE, not a ZIP. While some zipped (compressed) files do have the designation EXE, meaning they can be unzipped simply by double-clicking them, this one is far too small to contain even one photograph:

```
Subj: Fwd: IF YOU LIKE PORN DOWNLOAD THIS
Date: 97-06-03 18:05:13 EDT
From: PestUser
To: YourName

File: XXXPORN.EXE (26637 bytes)
DL Time (28800 bps): < 1 minute
```

When you look at the various types of password phishing, you can see they're not that clever. They rely on a victim's ignorance, not on the phisher's brilliance. The best way to foil these scams is to be aware of them. Don't download from someone you don't know. Especially don't download an executable file from someone you don't know. If you use an automatic program to pick up your Email, do not allow it to automatically download files.

Don't answer any request for your password through instant message, DCC chat, onscreen or Email. No one will ever have a legitimate need for your password.

Don't answer any request for your password through instant message, DCC chat, onscreen or Email. No one will ever have a legitimate need for your password. It's like the PIN number on your bank ATM card. Surely, if a stranger asked for your PIN and your bank card, you wouldn't hand it over! If you give your password out to anyone, you've done basically the same thing as handing them your bank card and PIN.

185

Safety On The Net

Chapter 8

The only time you may be asked for your password is if you dial in to your ISP's customer service, you may be required to give it for account identification. In this case, give the person your password. You dialed into them, you know they're the real folks!

Carding

Carding is an illegal activity which also relies on the ignorance of the victim as opposed to the brilliance of the thief. In carding, the thief acquires the user's credit card number, then usually has goods, paid for with the stolen card, shipped to a rented apartment or empty house. The items can then be resold to the thief's profit. Meanwhile, the card holder is usually only responsible for a small portion of the debt and the cardholder's bank eats the main cost of the crime.

Like your password, no one has a legitimate need to ask you for your credit card number except in those few exceptions when you are purchasing items online. When purchasing anything online, make sure you are using a secured browser which has encryption enabled. You can tell if you are by checking the manufacturer's documentation, but as a general rule, Microsoft Internet Explorer, Netscape Navigator and AOL's browsers are all capable of encryption. Also, any area on an ISP set up for commerce will have secured means to submit a credit card number, and some will allow you to charge the purchase to your ISP account balance.

> *Your ISP has no need to request your credit card number while you're logged on if you're not engaged in a purchase.*

Do not answer any request for your credit card number that doesn't come from one of those sources. Your ISP has no need to request your credit card number while you are logged on if you are not engaged in a purchase. They will not send you a

Safety On The Net

Chapter 8

DCC or instant message, nor will they request you go to a site on the World Wide Web and submit your credit card there.

Again, think of it as if a stranger approached you in your local department store and requested you hand them your credit card, since they were an authorized representative of the store and needed to verify it. I don't think too many folks would fall for that.

Warez

Pirates aren't out roaming the seven seas with peg legs and black eye patches, talking to parrots perched on their shoulders and firing cannon rounds at passing ships. No, pirates on the seas of cyberspace are stealing money from software authors and companies by retransmitting software for a reduced price when they have no license to give. *Warez* is the same thing as pirating, it's just a different word for the same criminal act. If you read the typical fine print on a software package when you open it, you'll probably find something like the following:

> 1. Grant of License. <company name> grants to you a non-exclusive, non-transferable license to install and use the Software on your computer. Such license grant is conditioned upon the following limitations: (i) copies of the Software may be made for backup and archival purposes only; (ii) you do not reverse engineer, decompile or disassemble the software; and (iii) you do not use the Software for purposes other than as authorized in this end user agreement or knowingly permit anyone else to do so.

In plain English, that means you agree to only install the software on your computer, not to make copies of it and not to attempt to decode it for your own use. There are felony punitive measures exacted against those who:

Safety On The Net

Chapter 8

> willfully and for the purposes of commercial advantage or private financial gain," 17 U.S.C. § 506 (a), reproduce or distribute, during any 180-day period, "at least 10 copies . . . of 1 or more copyrighted works, with a retail value of more than $2500." 18 U.S.C. § 2319 (b) (1). The numerical threshold exists, according to the legislative history, to exclude from felony prosecution "children making copies for friends as well as other incidental copying of copyrighted works having a relatively low retail value." H.R. Rep. No. 997, 102 Cong., 2d Sess., at 6 (Oct. 3, 1992).

In other words, don't do it! If you're approached asking to "trade" commercial software, or send files from your commercial software to a stranger, you may be letting yourself in for some severe consequences. If a person needs a particular file and they have a valid reason for needing it, they can get it from the software's producer.

Cracking

The second half of the end user license agreement quoted above states that the licensee agrees not to attempt to decode the software. This is called *cracking*. Usually, this is done to steal the code of the software so it can be duplicated. However, some crackers also decode sections of common ISP front end software in order to cause disruptions. This kind of cracking is done just to make a pain of oneself, as they manipulate the software to create forbidden screen names, screen names that don't show up in rooms, create false text to appear by someone else's screen name and so on.

Cracking is a violation of the software's license agreement and is a punishable felony. Although you probably don't intend to start cracking software codes in the near future, you do need to be sure you don't possess one of these cracked pieces of software. If someone offers you one, decline. Again, this is a felony, and if somehow you end up implicated in a crime of this sort, you want to be sure you don't have the evidence sitting on your hard drive!

Safety On The Net

Chapter 8

Remember that deleting is not enough to remove all signs of a software package, secure deleting is not enough and in some instances, even drives that have been formatted can still have old data retrieved off them. Even removing the FAT table is sometimes not enough to thwart sophisticated decoding and recovering programs. The best way to keep from getting entangled in this crime is to have nothing to do with it, no matter how enticing it may sound or how low the odds of getting caught may seem.

Phishing, carding, pirating and cracking are just not worth the fines and possible jail time that accompanies them when you get found out.

Wormers

Our next pests are *wormers*, who write virus programs. Worms are programs that corrupt the data in a file. Like a worm in an apple, the outside of the file appears fine. The data within, however, is irretrievable. Some programs may even run on an infected machine, but saving the output is pointless. Unfortunately, you can't tell that you have a worm until your data starts disappearing.

> *The best way to foil a wormer is by not downloading anything from anyone you don't know. Another way is to be sure you're using a safe web browser, like Netscape Navigator or Microsoft Internet Explorer.*

Worming is also a felony, depending on the value of the damage lost. If a worm gets into a network and destroys several hundred irreplaceable database files, for instance, you could be responsible for million of dollars!

The best way to foil a wormer is by not downloading anything from anyone you don't know. Another way to be sure you don't fall victim to one of these pests is to

Safety On The Net

Chapter 8

be sure you're using a safe web browser, like Netscape Navigator or Microsoft Internet Explorer.

You need to be sure to use a browser that alerts you when you are downloading a file and which can filter out a virus hidden in HTML coding, which is what web pages are constructed with. Web site viruses are rare, but they do exist. Any reputable browser will not allow this kind of harmful coding to get through. Recently Microsoft found Internet Explorer had a leak in it that would allow a certain type of harmful code to get through. Microsoft has made the necessary repairs and the fix is easily obtainable through them.

Another good preventative measure for keeping a wormer from hurting your system is to keep adequate and updated virus protection on your computer. These programs are easily found at any software outlet, usually running from $50 to $100 dollars, with free updates for a period of 1 to 3 years. Set these to load when you start your computer, so anything that may have slipped aboard during your last online session won't launch and do it's damage. It does very little good to run a virus scan at shutoff, since many of these programs have to be loaded before they run, and shutting down the computer rarely does that.

Cyberpunks

The next set of pests aren't really dangerous, but they can be annoying. These are the *cyberpunks*. By themselves, their actions are generally not harmful. They scroll and flood. They send vulgarity to screen. They go on rampages to clear the cyberworld of any restrictions. They may have annoying webs sites advocating the eradication of any kind of Internet parental or governmental control.

Safety On The Net

Chapter 8

Usually, using "/ignore" or the ignore feature on the proprietary service's front end is enough to rid yourself of a cyberpunk. However, when they decide to take their vendettas against you, it can be a bother. Usually, you will find these types on the proprietary services.

Your average cyberpunk is a male between the ages of 16 and 25, in school and fairly literate. They are the modern disenchanted youth, out of high school or will be soon and wavering in the real world/college world void.

Their goal is to be a hero in the cyberworld, since the real world has sort of been a let down for them. They may send you mailbombs, which are hundreds of useless letters that fill your mailbox, or they may send you instant message bombs, which are hundreds of useless instant messages. Minimizing an instant message bomb instead of canceling it will render it useless. Deleting a mail bomb is the best way to get rid of one of those.

> *Their goal is to be a hero in the cyberworld. They may send you mailbombs (hundreds of useless letters filling your mailbox) or instant message bombs (hundreds of useless instant messages).*

Under no circumstances should you reply to one of these folks. That's giving them attention, which is what they're after. Don't give them what they want, and they will sooner or later go away. There's no good single way to keep from getting a cyberpunk's attention in the first place, since what they're fighting against is a system, not a particular person, and you don't know if you're that person until it happens. The best defense against a cyberpunk is your old faithful ignore, which makes them go away on your screen, and eventually they do get the hint and move on to better targets.

Safety On The Net

Chapter 8

Phreakers

Phreakers aren't anyone who will get in your way too much online either, but you do need to be sure that you don't give them any kind of personal information which may help them. Phreakers are people who use hardware devices known as "boxes" to bilk money out of long-distance phone companies. In some instances, the boxes emit tones that the company's computer reads as an access code to allow long-distances calls.

In other cases, phreakers will route their long-distance charges through another number. All you need to protect yourself is to make sure that a phreaker never has access to your telephone number. How? The easiest way is to never give your telephone number online to someone you don't know.

You will never know (in person) some of the people that you meet online. However long you chat with someone online, even if it's years, you will never truly know that person is who or what they claim to be. However, after a few weeks, you can generally tell if it's someone who's using you to get information for a criminal activity or if it's someone who is being genuinely friendly.

> *All you need to protect yourself is to make sure that a phreaker never has access to your telephone number. How? The easiest way is to never give your telephone number online to someone you don't know.*

After you've established that, it's easy to say that this may be someone to whom it is safe to give your phone number for a "live" chat. One of the peculiarities of online chat is that it can seem easy to become intimately acquainted with someone in a matter of hours. This is no more true online than it is in real life, but because of the nature of the medium, many people are fooled into thinking

Safety On The Net

Chapter 8

they know someone a lot better than they do after a short period of time. Being aware of this will help you to maintain a safe distance until you've had enough time to truly get to know a new friend.

Online allows you to filter out a lot of negative things, and you may not be aware of a person's more unsavory traits until it's too late (too late is when a phreaker is using your telephone number to dial up Zaire)!

The online pests you will come into contact with the most are hackers, whackers and wannabes. It's very important to distinguish between these three groups. A true hacker lives his online life by the hacker's ethic. According to the hacker ethic, all technical information should, in principle, be freely available to all. Gaining entry to a system to explore data and increase knowledge is never unethical, therefore. But, destroying, altering or moving data in such a way that could cause injury or expense to others is always unethical. Unfortunately, the media have applied the term to anyone online who is engaging in potentially illegal activities. A hacker will never bother you online.

Whacker

A *whacker*, on the other hand, will bother you and anyone else he can find. Shortened from wannabe-hacker, a whacker is a person who invades systems and security strictly to do damage. These thieves create simplistic programs using Visual Basic (an easily obtained lower level programming language sold in a box), then distribute these programs to wannabes and cyberpunks free of charge. The wannabes and the cyberpunks are easy targets of this class, because they want to be on a quest or a crusade.

A wannabe is a person who wants to whack, but doesn't have the technical expertise (see below). Whackers are going to be responsible for most of your warez trading, Email bombing assistance, IM

Safety On The Net

Chapter 8

bombing programs, etc. Recently, a whacker was indicted and sent to jail for creating a program that generated fake credit card numbers for the purpose of creating numerous AOL accounts, which were used to invade chat rooms and forums and disrupt the other users.

Like cyberpunks and other disrupters online, the best way to be rid of a whacker is to ignore him or her. The problem with reporting these people to the online service is that, as before, they're after attention. The online service can cancel the account, but the whacker will usually just make another, and now he's been fed what he wanted. So he goes after you again under a new name and a dreary circle is created.

I have been in situations where a room ignored a whacker, who got angrier and angrier, trying every trick in the book. They scrolled, they flooded, they swore, they IM bombed, they Email bombed. They threatened and ranted. They came in and out of the room to break everyone's ignore. They also eventually went away. I've also been in situations where the room either paged for outside help or took it on themselves to rid themselves of the pest. Those people came back over and over, totally disrupting the room. They had 23 members' undivided attention. As soon as one account was canceled, back they came on a new one. It's not too hard to tell who won that war.

> *Like cyberpunks and other disrupters online, the best way to be rid of a whacker is to ignore him or her. When you allow them to manipulate you into fighting back, they've won.*

The lesson here is to ignore these people. They aren't worth the expense of your monthly membership to an ISP and your registration fee for your IRC program. When you allow them to manipulate you into fighting back, they've won.

Safety On The Net

Chapter 8

Wannabe

Wannabes are pretty much the same as whackers, only they lack the ability to whack themselves. You'll find them in the public chat rooms on AOL, mostly making a nuisance of themselves. They rarely have the means to create multiple accounts, usually have very little clue how to use most of the features of the whacker software they have, and are generally not that exciting.

Ignoring a wannabe works even better than ignoring a whacker because this is a person who doesn't even have the skills required to be a pain on their own. As these people get more mature in their online skills, you may find them turning into cyberpunks or creating web pages with potentially harassing material on them.

Online stalkers

The last pests are the online stalkers: people who get attached to you for some reason and will not leave you alone, no matter how little interest you display. These people will sometimes go so far as to get your home address and telephone number and come visit you or call you.

The problem with stalkers, besides the obvious, is that when you rebuff them, they can turn ugly, and their love letters turn threatening. They may post personal information about you, or lies about you, they may inundate you with Email and IMs, and they may go so far as to attempt physical violence against you if you are careless enough to give out your name and number online. This is one reason why it is so very important not to immediately trust anyone you meet online.

Safety On The Net

Chapter 8

There are some things you can do to stop an online stalker. First, be aware that not all insistent correspondence is stalking. When it gets to be several unwanted emails a day, or several unwanted DCC chats, or you find them in every room you enter and every channel you play on, then you can start to consider it stalking.

It may go on for several months, or in some cases years, depending on the type of person involved. Watch for certain types of key elements to mails, which are usually unsolicited. Unfortunately, even not responding to this type of person may not make them go away.

Things to look for in Email and chat from this kind of person include:

- Threats

- Pledges of undying love

- A sense of being betrayed by the victim

- Use of personal information you haven't provided (your name, your family's names, place where you work, address, etc.)

- A deal to stop harassment if you will "love" the person

- Persistent presence of the person when you have asked to be left alone

The following is an example of the kind of messages you may receive. These are actual messages received by the victim of an online stalker. As she refuses to answer, the stalker becomes angrier. This person eventually sent a mailing containing the victim's home telephone number to over 100 people. The harassment stopped when the victim sought a restraining order against the stalker, who sent over 400 pieces of Email to the victim:

Safety On The Net

Chapter 8

Harasser:	guess what
Harasser:	well besides the fact that you refuse to talk to me
Harasser:	well neverdamnmind
Harasser:	you know how much i hate being ignored by you
Harasser:	i think that's why you do it so much
Harasser:	ok, now I'm pissed
Harasser:	I cannot handle this (deleted)..it makes me sick!
Harasser:	<— — is reaching level 3, which involves mass mail and any other online warfare possibly containing damaging information on the subject!

If you have a person bothering you who seems to be a stalker, you can do several things. First, forward all materials and mailings, including yours asking that contact cease, to the owner of the proprietary service or ISP you use to get online. Keep all this material backed up in a safe place in case you do need to take your stalker to court.

Check on stalking laws in your state to find out how to start a case against a potential stalker. Some states require several weeks of verification before you can begin any kind of proceedings.

If you know the person involved by name, you can protect yourself physically by getting a restraining order against that person. A *restraining order* is a document that prevents a person from coming within a certain distance of you, your home or your family. Contact your police department to let them know this is happening if you are receiving telephone calls or mail at your home.

Most importantly, check with an attorney to find out how your state's stalking laws work. Since every state is different we cannot give you every detail on what constitutes stalking in your area.

Safety On The Net

Chapter 8

As with the other types of online pests, forewarned is forearmed. The best prevention against this harassment becoming dangerous is to know how to protect yourself in advance. This is not a common thing that happens online, but it does occur, and to keep it from happening to you, you need to know how to best combat it.

Physical Security

Physical security relates to two different types of activities involved with being online. One of them is the machinery you have to get you there, your computer and your ISP account. The other is meeting people in person whom you have met online. I'm going to outline some steps to make both of these secure and safer.

Your computer and your ISP account are the most valuable assets you have in the online world. If your online connection is at work, you may need to take extra precautions to make sure no one tampers with your computer.

Passwords and physical security measures

Your computer needs to be protected with passwords and physical security measures. Use a BIOS password and a Windows 95 operating password. A BIOS password is usually controlled with a physical change of pins on a card inside the machine, called a jumper. In addition to setting this jumper, you need to be sure to lock the faceplate of the machine, so no one can just open it and remove the physical switch. Directions on how to set a BIOS password should be included in your computer's documentation.

Safety On The Net

Chapter 8

Make your password as long as possible (at least ten characters). This is the same for your ISP account's password. Don't use something obvious, like swear words or your birthday. Change your password monthly. Never write your password down near your computer. Remember it, or keep it in your wallet or at home. Don't have your account's name and your password on the same sheet of paper.

If you take your machine to be repaired, use Add/Remove Programs to remove AOL. Your password is contained in a file on your hard drive called Main.IDX. If you leave this file on your computer, anyone who knows how to get the information off your drive can have access to your account. It's easier to reinstall the America Online software than it is to pay for the damages caused by letting your account be compromised. If you forget to remove AOL, check your "mail sent" area for any mail you didn't send. If you find any, run a virus scan over your machine immediately and change your password.

If you have to leave your place of employment and you don't have the opportunity to remove AOL, change your password as soon as you can, to prevent compromise of the account by a future user of your equipment. When you've changed your password, don't go back to one you've used before. Use a new one each time.

You can also make physical changes to the contents of your hard drive which will make it harder for worm and HTML viruses to cause damage. Go to the DOS directory and remove the following programs to a floppy disk, taking them completely off your system:

Safety On The Net

Chapter 8

Command	Function/Purpose
FORMAT	The format of floppy disks and hard drives is the magnetic pattern laid down by a formatting utility.
DELTREE	Deletes a directory and all it's subdirectories
SUBST	Substitutes variable or a word for a command
JOIN	Combines two files
BACKUP	Backs up your data
RESTORE	Restores data saved in a backup
ATTRIB	Change the attribution of files, how they can be manipulated

This will prevent some worms from running, as they won't be able to call upon those commands. In addition, you'll get a warning that this file can't be found, or "bad command or file name," which will tip you off that you need to run a virus scanner over your hard drive before proceeding. Windows 95 doesn't need these commands in order to run, and you can save yourself some heartache by putting them someplace besides the DOS directory where they're easy for a worm to find.

Safety in meeting people from online

When you've met some people online and spoken to them for a while, have gotten to know them and become friends with them, you may want to meet offline for some face to face interaction. While this is not a bad idea, it is wise to remember that even if you've spoken to someone online for several years, they still may not be who you think they are.

Therefore, you want to use some basic safety precautions when meeting someone offline for the first time. Don't be afraid to insist on these things. It's much more important to be safe than to not offend someone. If a person you want to meet offline is not agreeable to these terms, they may not be someone you really should be

Safety On The Net

Chapter 8

meeting, for your own safety. While the odds of running into a Ted Bundy online are a long shot, you are always better safe than sorry when it comes to your life, safety and well being.

These recommendations may seem elementary in their commonsensical nature, but there may be one or two items here you haven't considered, or that didn't occur to you as being necessary for a safe and enjoyable offline experience with your online friends. I know folks online who met their future spouses and best friends online first, so don't look at this as unusual, just as being better safe than sorry!

Meet in a public place

If you agree to meet someone offline, don't go to their home. Instead, meet in a public place. Go to a restaurant, a large club, a disco, Shakespeare in the Park or some other area with other people around. Don't go to a secluded area or someplace unfamiliar. Find some mutually known location and arrange to meet there. Don't arrange to meet someplace that involves being in a dark or hard to escape from area, like an alley, a small club or a car in a small park.

Meet in a group

If possible, arrange to meet in a group. Some folks like to have "bashes" or parties where they all meet in a public place as a group and go do something. These bashes can sometimes resemble conferences, as they are held in large hotels with banks of computers set up for folks to check Email and chat with friends who are unable to attend. If you go to one of these bashes, expect to be called by your screen name, as you'll most likely be wearing it on your chest in the form of a name tag. Bashes offer a fun and affordable way to meet many of your online friends at the same time in a safe environment.

Safety On The Net

Chapter 8

Give yourself time to cultivate an actual friendship

Don't agree to meet someone you have only known a couple of days. Give yourself some time to cultivate an actual friendship before assuming that someone you've met online is a friend. As I said before, online chats can foster a false sense of intimacy, and you may be totally off the mark in your judgment of a person you meet here. They may seem to totally fit your mold of the perfect soulmate, but they may be a scam artist who has read enough of your profile and talked to you long enough to play the role of what you're looking for very well. Remember that this is what scammers do the best, pretend to be someone else. If you give enough personal information about your likes and dislikes, anyone with a little bit of skill in people relations and a keen sense of deduction can appear to be whoever you want them to be.

Let someone know where you are

Finally, make sure that someone knows where you're going and when you intend to be back. Then be back at that time. Give them a phone number to reach you .If you're planning on staying longer than you had anticipated, give them a call and let them know. Under no circumstances go out without letting someone know where you'll be. If something was to happen and you were to disappear, the sooner someone knows and can notify the authorities, the better it will be.

The preceding isn't meant to scare anyone, or to over dramatize. Just be aware and you'll have no trouble at all. There's a fascinating world of new people out there—all you need to do is exercise a little care so the bad ones aren't the ones you meet!

The End

Chapter 9

The Beatles have a song called "The End," as do the Doors, although they're far ends of the spectrum from one another as to the message they portray about endings.

In this ending I want to recap what we've done, look to what we can do, and sum it all up in a condensed, easy-to-remember format.

The best way to do this is with my 10 Commandments of Online Chat. These rules are an easy way to get the most out of your online time.

1. Know your basics

By knowing the basic ideas of how your computer and online communication work, you can pick the best method for you, and do your own troubleshooting.

The End

Chapter 9

2. Know the lingo

Keeping up with how folks are talking online can help you understand faster, fit in easier and follow conversations better. The more you talk the talk and walk the walk, the faster you'll be accepted.

3. Know the rules

No one wants to look like a fool because they don't know the basic rules of the game! Read the rules when you log on, respect them and follow them. The online services and ISPs you log on to invite you in as a guest, so treat their homes with courtesy and respect.

4. Lurk before you leap

Learn the culture of a room by observing it. By watching, you can find out what is expected and what's crass in a channel before you leap into the conversation.

5. Know the unwritten rule

Treat others as you'd like to be treated.

6. Educate those around you

Don't just get upset when someone breaks one of the rules or one of your personal boundaries! Take the initiative to help educate that person. They may simply not know any better.

7. Participate

Don't wait to be noticed in a room or on a channel, make yourself and your presence known. Online is no place to be a wallflower.

The End

Chapter 9

8. Be you

You're the person these others want to get to know. Almost everyone's read Harlequin romances and fairy tales, so we don't need to get to know those people again. We want to meet you!

9. Empower yourself

Don't run to the sysops and AOL volunteers every time someone does something you don't like. Learn to ignore, learn to use kick and ban, and learn most of all how to have fun without letting the occasional pest get in your way. When you take control of your online experience, you can make it exactly what you want it to be.

10. Have fun

Be safe, take control, but never forget, the purpose of this is to have a good time and learn to communicate with many different people. Don't lose sight of that and become engrossed in small-time online soap operas and sad stories. Be a positive, not a negative aspect in the online experiences of those you encounter.

The World Wide Web links all its participants together. The same can be said for the larger Internet and for the world of online chat. Remember that how you act affects someone else, who in turn affects another person. As the nursery rhyme goes, "For want of a nail, the kingdom fell," so be sure you're contributing as positively as you can. It's a great big world out there—welcome!

Appendix A: Glossary

Appendix A: Glossary

AOL Terms of Service

The set of rules which you must follow to maintain membership in America Online

Ban

An IRC command that permanently removes a user from the chat area.

Bandwidth

A measure of the frequency, expressed in cycles per second (Hertz) or bits per second (bps), at which a channel can transfer information.

Buffers

A portion of memory allocated for temporarily storing information about a computing task.

Byte

One digital character (a zero or a one).

Channel

A "room" or chat area on an IRC server.

Client

The software one uses to access an IRC server.

Glossary

Appendix A

CPU
Central Processing Unit—the main brain of the computer

CUSeeMe
A video chat client for use on the WWW.

Cyberspace
The boundless virtual realm where all online transactions occur, including chat, telephone and Web surfing.

DCC
Direct Channel Chat—bypassing an IRC network and connecting directly to another IRC client.

Default
A predefined setting in an application.

Desktop
The part of your computer's operating system you see when no other applications are running.

Downloading
Copying a file from another computer attached to the Internet to your computer.

Emoticons
Simple drawings created by standard text characters that are used to express emotions in online chat. Also called "smileys."

FAQ
Frequently Asked Questions—a text file that answers the questions commonly asked by new users.

Glossary

Appendix A

Firewall
A security procedure that places a specially programmed computer system between an organization's internal network and the Internet, protecting the former from access by unauthorized users.

Flame
A nasty, unnecessary message usually sent with malicious intent, frequently vulgar.

FTP
File Transfer Protocol—the most common protocol for downloading files.

GUI
Graphic User Interface—an interface for working with computers based on visual icons (such as Macintosh OS or Windows).

Hardware
The physical machinery of your computer.

Ignore
An IRC command that blocks a users chat from appearing on your screen.

Instant Messages
Small private messages sent from one user to another on AOL.

Internet
A worldwide network of computers.

IRC
Internet Relay Chat—one system for communicating with other people via the Internet.

Kick
An IRC command that removes a user from a chat area.

Glossary

Appendix A

Minimize
To reduce an application to an icon or button on the computer's desktop.

mIRC
One of the most popular IRC clients

Modem
Modulator/Demodulator—a hardware device that translates between a computer's digital language and the analog system used by telephone lines, allowing you to connect to the Internet or another computer through ordinary phone lines.

MOO
MUD Object Oriented—a lexical variation of MUD

MUD
Multi-User Dungeon/Dimension—a genre of imagination-fueled role-playing games based on the Internet.

MUSH
Multi-User Shared Hallucination—another lexical variation of MUD.

Netiquette
A set of customs for interacting via the Internet. "Network" + "etiquette".

Newbie
A person who is new to a particular computing environment.

Password sniffer
A program which can detect a user's password and send it to an unauthorized user.

Peripheral
A piece of computer hardware that is not essential to the computer's operation.

Glossary

Appendix A

Persona
An online character adopted in chat-based games (frowned upon in most other chat areas.

Pictograph
A symbol similar to an emoticon.

Ping
Packet Internet Groper—a diagnostic utility program commonly used to check a computer's connection to the Internet.

Port
An interface which governs the flow of information over a channel.

Proprietary service
A private, commercial Internet service provider.

RAM
Random Access Memory—the buffer capacity of your computer, measured in megabytes.

Root Directory
The starting directory of an application.

Screen name
The nickname one chooses when joining an IRC channel or other online venue.

Server
The computer where an application is resident; on the Internet or the Web it refers to the computer that stores Web sites or accepts commands for downloads.

Glossary

Appendix A

Shareware
A program which can be used for an evaluation period. Continued use after this evaluation period requires a license (and usually a small fee).

Shorthands
Common abbreviations used in place of words or phrases.

Software
Applications used on your computer.

Spam
A mysterious meat (?) product; Also, unsolicited (usually commercial) messages sent through Email or to chat areas.

Telnet
A communications protocol used to access some chat and MUD areas.

Upgrade
An update to your software, making it the most recent version of the product.

World Wide Web (or Web)
The graphic portion of the Internet.

Winsock
A file which allows a Windows computer to access TCP/IP connections.

Zipped file
A file which has been compressed to occupy less space on disk or for faster file transfers.

Appendix B: Companion CD-ROM Contents

Appendix B: Companion CD-ROM Contents

The following table lists and explains the directories and contents that you'll find on the companion CD-ROM:

Directory	Contents
ABACUS	Contains the electronic version of the Abacus Book & Software Catalog.
ATCHAT10	AtChat from Abbott Systems, Inc.
AWB	ActiveWorlds from Worlds, Inc.
CU30	CU-SeeMe Version 3.0 from White Pine Software, Inc.
CUSESS	CU-SeeMe Accessories from White Pine Software, Inc.
FERRET	NetFerret and IRCFerret from FerretSoft LLC.
ICIE222	ichat 32-bit plug-in chat utility from ichat, Inc.
LOLCHAT	Chat software from LOL Software, Inc.
MASQ140	Masquerade from HiJiNX Interactive Enterprises, Inc.
MIRCSO2T	mIRC from Khaled Mardam-Bey and mIRC Co., LTD.
NETGAMMON	Play Backgammon from GOTO.
PAGER	ichat Inc.'s Internet Pager evaluation.
POW WOW	and Kids' Pow Wow, personal communication chat software from Tribal Voice, Inc.
WPB	White Pine Software, Inc.'s WhitePine Board evaluation.
ZMUD	Zugg's Multi-User Dungeon Internet Software.
	Additional files including AT&T's WorldNet and CompuServe's Sprynet internet services sign-up programs.

Companion CD-ROM Contents

Appendix B

For more complete details on installing the companion CD-ROM, see Chapter 1.

AtChat

AtChat is copyright Abbott Systems Inc.

AtChat is *serverless* chat. It allows you to chat directly with virtually anyone on the Internet at anytime. To locate someone, all you need is their Email address. AtChat doesn't use any central servers so there is no "list of users" and nobody is "logged on" (there is nothing to log onto).

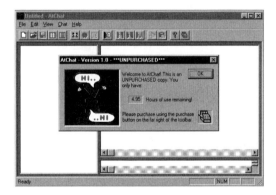

The benefits of serverless chat are:

- ❖ Your privacy is protected since no registration is involved.
- ❖ Nothing to fail or slow you down since no central server is involved.
- ❖ A low one-time purchase price (no monthly fees).
- ❖ No advertising to distract you or clutter your screen.

AtChat is a private and not public chat. It's designed for private personal chat or business chat applications. Because it doesn't have "lists of users" or "people logged on," AtChat isn't designed for social or public chat. In other words, you cannot meet people on AtChat. If you're looking for this type of chat, many free solutions offered by online services, Web sites, IRC, etc., are available.

219

Companion CD-ROM Contents

Appendix B

AtChat uses Email to make connections and only uses Email addresses to find people. Once the person is found, AtChat sets up a direct Internet connection for the actual chat. This direct connection is IP-IP and is fast and private. AtChat doesn't work with AOL. AtChat uses industry standard POP3 email. AOL, and some other services, use their own proprietary email systems. Unfortunately, AtChat cannot work with these systems.

Because AtChat is *text* chat, it doesn't support voice or video but you can send files to anyone with whom you are chatting and even continue chatting while the file is sent in the background. AtChat also supports group chat. You can easily host a group chat with several people (a great idea for meetings).

Also, both people must have AtChat running to chat. You can leave it running while you do other tasks and it will notify you when a chat request comes in. You can even choose the type of notification—play a sound, flash the menu bar, bring the window to front or any combination.

AtChat supports test chat so if your friends are busy, you can test chat with Abbott Systems anytime. Simply send a chat request to the following address:

```
beta@abbottsys.com
```

If they're too busy, their friendly chat robot, Robbie, will chat with you. AtChat is available in a free, full-featured, time-limited version. Since they're currently testing this version, don't panic if you see "purchase" screens.

For more information

Abbott Systems

1-800-552-9157 or 914-747-4201
Fax: 914-747-9115
Email: info@abbottsys.com
Web: http://www.abbottsys.com

Companion CD-ROM Contents

Appendix B

Active Worlds

Active Worlds is copyright © by Worlds, Inc.

AlphaWorld may be the first Active World you'll visit. It allows you to build and claim property and retain ownership of that property. Note that some of the other Active Worlds have their permissions set differently. Some Active Worlds won't let you build and others require a special entry code before you are allowed to enter or build.

Active Worlds Browser is a program that you use to visit Active Worlds' virtual environments. An Active World is a place that you inhabit with other users who are logged in to the Active World at the same time as you are. You can communicate with other users and you can see their avatars.

Many Active Worlds let you build, and whatever you build is visible to all others who visit that Active World. The location and specifics of the objects that you place are sent to the Active WorldServer. In short, an Active World is a shared experience using the Active Worlds Browser as an intermediary and common language.

You start by immigrating to the Active World. To do this, you'll need to launch the Active Worlds Browser program and get a citizenship ID number. Then complete the dialog box and the next time you launch Active Worlds Browser you'll be a citizen. Then you can start exploring and building.

Companion CD-ROM Contents

Appendix B

Read the Help file if you have questions. To do this, click the Contents button. This displays a list of topics you can select or use the Search button to search by keyword. You can also get additional information by asking other users, checking their web pages (http://www.activeworlds.com) or joining their newsgroups.

Each Active World may be subtly or radically different, but the Browser can take you to all of them. As the Web-of-Worlds expands, your Active Worlds Browser can take you from place to place quickly and easily, and you'll be able to see new places and talk to new people.

For more information

Circle of Fire Studios, Inc.
6150 Yarrow Dr. Ste. G
Carlsbad, CA 92009

760-431-4332 or 760-431-4333
Fax: 760-431-4330
http://www.activeworlds.com

CU-See Me

CU-SeeMe is copyright © 1997 White Pines Software, Inc.

CU-SeeMe is White Pine's award-winning Internet video chat software for interacting with others using full color video, audio, typed text and whiteboard communications. Now you too can meet new people, expand your professional and social networks and do more with CU-SeeMe.

CU-SeeMe is the leading software for video chat. It can be used over the Internet or any other TCP/IP network. By using CU-SeeMe, you can make new friends, expand your professional and social networks, find people with similar interests, watch entertaining cybercast events and more.

Companion CD-ROM Contents

Appendix B

CU-SeeMe is easy-to-use. It includes an online directory to locate other CU-SeeMe users and a list of public Reflector sites for live group interaction. You can even create and control your own conference using CU-SeeMe with White Pine's Reflector&trade software. Visit the CU-SeeMe Web page (http://www.cuseeme.com) to find out about new and exciting events being cybercast over the Internet.

CU-SeeMe is a community. People all over the world are building social networks using the power of CU-SeeMe. It's software for everyone; you too will be saying "CU on the Net".

White Pine Software was also kind enough to include their award winning demonstration software accessories which include CU-Doodle, CU-Dial and FaceIt.

For more information

White Pine Software, Inc.
542 Amherst Street
Nashua, NH 03063

603-886-9050
Fax: 603-886-9051
Email: info@wpine.com
www.cu-seeme.com or www.wpine.com

IRCFerret & WebFerret

IRCFerret & WebFerret are copyright © 1997 FerretSoft LLC

WebFerret is the easiest way to locate the information that you want on the Internet. WebFerret queries large Web search engines to find what you are looking for on the World Wide Web. It will query all configured search engines simultaneously and discards any duplicate results. Results that are returned (often within two seconds) can be acted upon immediately. New Search engines are added automatically to the application as they become available. WebFerret is available free and forms part of the NetFerret suite of search utilities. If you find WebFerret useful, you can buy it along with the full NetFerret suite of search utilities.

Companion CD-ROM Contents

Appendix B

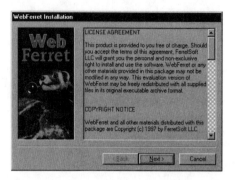

IRCFerret, another member of the NetFerret Suite, will search the IRC networks around the world. Searches are specified by the keywords you enter, matching them against every IRC user's host address, nickname, and description. You can even limit specific channels to search.

The IRC networks will be searched simultaneously, without you having to manually connect and search yourself. Searches are done intelligently and efficiently to save you time and bandwidth. Once the search results have been returned, you can (if you have an IRC client installed) join the channel with the user you have selected, and start chatting.

Alternatively, IRCFerret lets you mail the user, using your MAPI mail client (e.g., Microsoft Exchange), or save the user's email address into your MAPI address book. If the user has his Web page URL in his description (common practice), IRCFerret lets you launch your Web browser and automatically takes you to the user's Web page.

For more information

FerretSoft LLC
1209 Hill Road North
Suite 109
Pickerington, Ohio 43147

614-755-3891
Email sales@ferretsoft.com
http://www.ferretsoft.co

224

Companion CD-ROM Contents

Appendix B

ichat

ichat is copyright © by ichat, inc.

This easy-to-use plug-in, combined with the innovative ichat Interactive Server, brings real-time chat to the World Wide Web. The ichat Active-X Control Internet Explorer Web Browser version 2.2 allows users to surf the World Wide Web and chat online at the same time. The ichat Browser Control features seamless integration with Internet Explorer. Or, if you are using Netscape's Navigator, ichat has included their outstanding plug-in as well. Once installed, the ichat plug-in will automatically launch when you visit an ichat-served Web site.

The ichat Control is designed to access either standard IRC servers or the ichat Server. For IRC (Internet Relay Chat), click on any .chat file link. This will automatically activate the plug-in. Visit the ichat Web site (http://www.ichat.com) for more information on how to connect. To help ichat to serve you better, please report any bugs or e-mail comments or suggestions to support@ichat.com.

For more information

ichat, Inc. Corporate Headquarters
11100 Metric Blvd. Building 7
Austin, TX 78758 USA

512-425-2200
Fax: 512-719-8225
www.ichat.com

LOL Chat

LOL Chat is copyright © by LOL Software, Inc.

LOL lets you chat with 100 of your closest friends at once. You decide upon the limit. We cannot list all the features of this program so we suggest you simply try it.

Companion CD-ROM Contents

Appendix B

The following is just a short list of its features:

- ❖ Rich Text Formatting on the Fly—Text color, background color, font name & size, bold, italic, underline, and left, right, & center text justification.

- ❖ Password Protected Names—Change your name as often as you like.

- ❖ Custom Colors—Create your own colors for text and backgrounds.

- ❖ Copy & Paste—Paste in an URL, poem or an entire Word document with all its formatting.

- ❖ Multiple Servers—Jump between servers, call someone on a different server, or even search for someone across all servers.

- ❖ Run Your Own Server—Coming soon: run a server of your own, for everyone else to login to.

- ❖ Full Answering Machine—Leave a message for someone if they don't answer.

- ❖ Send Messages—to other people, even if they're on a different server. They can reply or save it in their Answering Machine.

- ❖ Multiple File Transfer to Multiple People—Send files to everyone, while receiving files from everyone!

- ❖ Custom Macros—Create hundreds for text, format changes, sounds, or any combination of the three.

Companion CD-ROM Contents

Appendix B

- ❖ Sound Manager—Auto-Load new sounds, drag-and-drop into folders.

- ❖ Address Manager—Customizable address book for keeping notes or doing quick searches across servers.

- ❖ Indicators and Status Messages—Notify you when someone doesn't have your sound, font, etc.

- ❖ Login List—View a list of people currently logged on to a server.

- ❖ User Info Pages—Create a mini-homepage to let people know about you or search for other people with the same interests.

- ❖ Pictures With Any Format and Size—Let people see what you look like.

Masquerade

Masquerade is copyright © by HiJiNX Interactive Entertainment

HiJiNX Masquerade is designed to provide a truly user-friendly communications program. Masquerade also aims to make communication over the Internet much more enjoyable by providing sight & sound—it allows you to see and hear the people you are talking to by using our proprietary PIX files and a Text To Speech (TTS) engine built into Masquerade. The result is animated images which synchronize with the voices from the speech engine.

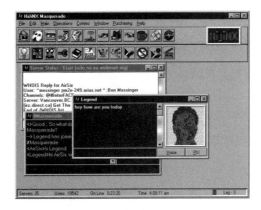

Companion CD-ROM Contents

Appendix B

Masquerade has the following features:

- ❖ Sight & Sound: Animation and TTS (text to speech) sound
- ❖ Send-a-Friend: This feature lets you tell your friends about Masquerade by e-mail
- ❖ Point & Click
- ❖ Animated Icons
- ❖ Configurable Window Colors
- ❖ Configurable Text Colors and fonts
- ❖ Easily configurable multi-level pop-up menus
- ❖ Logging on open and private conversations
- ❖ Secure Conversations and file transfers via Direct Computer Communication (DCC)

For more information:
HiJiNX Interactive Entertainment
P.O. Box 8303
Woolloongabba
Queensland Australia, 4102

Fax: +61-7-3844-8181
E-mail: info@hijinx.com.au
http://207.67.245.34/hijinx/

mIRC

mIRC is copyright © mIRC Co., LTD

mIRC v5.02, an Internet Relay Chat Client, provides a user-friendly interface for use with the Internet Relay Chat network. The IRC network is a virtual meeting place where people from all over the world can meet and talk. To IRC all you need to do is connect to a server, join a channel, and chat!

Companion CD-ROM Contents

Appendix B

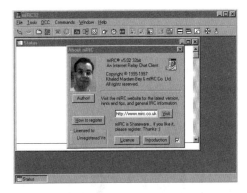

mIRC will guide you through these initial stages, and hopefully you'll be chatting in no time. If you get stuck or want to find out more about a certain feature, just click on a Help button (e.g., in the Setup dialog) and you should find some hints there to help you.

As you become more experienced you can also start configuring mIRC's features to suit your own needs and tastes, features such as colors, fonts, function keys, aliases, popup menus, scripts, sounds and many others. Remember to visit the mIRC homepage or one of it's mirror sites regularly for the latest version information, as well as for links to other mIRC and IRC related information and websites.

Visit their website at: www.mirc.com for more information.

NetGammon

NetGammon is copyright © by GOTO

Join the club today! It's easy: just download the free software, and connect yourself to the International Backgammon Server (IBS). Measure your abilities to play this exciting game against other International players of different ranks directly from your home. The server evaluates your performance after every game and you will have an up-to-date rating after each game. Even if you're a beginner, the friendly interface of the software will allow you to start your first game immediately, however, you can also read the beginners' rules for help.

Visit their website at http://ibs.nordnet.fr/netgammon/index_usa.html for more information.

Companion CD-ROM Contents

Appendix B

Pager

Pager is copyright © by ichat, Inc.

The ichat Pager is the fastest way to communicate on the Internet. The ichat Pager is your link to instant net-based communications.

Pager has the following features:

- Friends lists—The ichat Pager Friends wizard makes adding friends to your personal list quick and easy.

- Multiple user states—Tell at a glance when your friends are online, away from their computer, or if they do not want to be disturbed.

- Instant messages—Deliver NetPages instantly to anyone on the Internet.

- Quick chat—Initiate a chat with any number of friends and associates in a private conference room by sending a single message.

- File transfer—Drag a file onto a user's name to quickly send a document. Users receiving files have the option to accept or decline the sent file.

- Instant audio and video—Send links to any Real Media file to friends and associates and the ichat Pager will instantly launch the Real Player.

- Send URL—Easily share links to your favorite Web pages with your friends.

Companion CD-ROM Contents

Appendix B

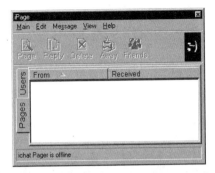

PowWow

PowWow is copyright © by Tribal Voice

PowWow is an unique Internet program for Windows that allows up to nine (9) people to chat, transfer files and cruise the Web together as a group. PowWow also has Communities (Chat Rooms), Text-to-Speech features and Email Answering Machine capabilities. NEW! PowWow now has Online Games, Bulletin Board Messaging for communities and more.

Contact Tribal Voice, Inc. at www.tribal.com for more information.

Companion CD-ROM Contents

Appendix B

PowWow for KIDS!

POWWOW for KIDS! is copyright © by Tribal Voice

Kids PowWow is a PowWow version strictly for children (up to age 13). It links with the PowWow for Kids home page and provides features that provide a protective environment for children who want to use PowWow. It alerts children when an adult pages them, or when they page an adult. The adult version of PowWow (versions 3.0+) will also display a warning to the user indicating that they are connected to a child.

The Kids home page provides a White Pages for children and children's conferences. The children's conferences have profanity filters to disallow the transmission of profanity in conference mode. To register as a PowWow kid, a valid email address must exist for the child. A registration password is given out through email and the password must be entered prior to using the program.

Contact Tribal Voice, Inc. at www.tribal.com for more information.

WhitePineBoard

WhitePineBoard is copyright © by White Pine Software, Inc.

What is WhitePineBoard? WhitePineBoard lets people in a conference view and make notes on their work over the network. It allows you to share and sketch out your ideas on an electronic markerboard. You can discuss things in a teleconference, starting from scratch or going over documents, spreadsheets, graphics and other types of applications.

Companion CD-ROM Contents

Appendix B

As you make the transition from conference table meetings to teleconferences, your document communication must evolve as well. It is no longer practical to sketch ideas on a markerboard because the markerboard is out of view of most of your colleagues. It is no longer practical to photocopy a document and pass it around the table as there is no table. WhitePineBoard replaces markerboards and photocopies and provides the medium for document communication in teleconferences. WhitePineBoard allows you to present your ideas and review documents electronically.

For more information

White Pine Software, Inc.
542 Amherst Street
Nashua, NH 03063

603-886-9050
Fax: 603-886-9051
Email: info@wpine.com
www.cu-seeme.com or www.wpine.com

The zMUD Connector (Zugg's Multi-User Dungeon)

The zMUD Connector (Zugg's Multi-User Dungeon) is copyright © (1994 - 96) by Andrew Cowan

zMUD allows you to connect to and play MUDs on the Internet, and provides you many useful tools, such as aliases, actions, macros, keys, buttons, scripts, maps, etc., to make your MUD life easier and more profitable. zMUD is available as a freeware version (v3.62a) which is not supported, and a shareware version (v4.1 and above) which continues to be regularly updated and improved. Support is available to registered users of the shareware version. The latest version of zMUD can be found at http://www.zuggsoft.com/zmud or in the TUCOWS Internet archive. Questions, suggestions, bug reports, etc. can be sent to Zugg at zugg@zuggsoft.com.

Companion CD-ROM Contents

Appendix B

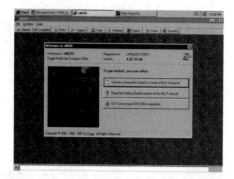

zMUD was designed based upon ideas from various versions of TINTIN, the popular UNIX MUD client. I have tried to provide compatibility with TINTIN so that users of that client will feel at home. However, since I have never actually used TINTIN myself, I cannot promise full compatibility. Concepts, functions and syntax are similar, but may differ. Of course, the graphical environment of Windows allows functions that were not possible in the text-based UNIX world, giving MUD players even more power. zMUD has been optimized for use on DIKU and LP combat MUDs. Since I don't play the social MUDs, zMUD may or may not be useful in those cases. However, in combat MUDs, zMUD excels, providing many mechanisms for outlaws, robots, etc.

zMUD has unique features for beginning MUD players, as well as for power wizards, builders and coders accustomed to clients like TINTIN. zMUD was developed and tested as both a 16-bit and 32-bit Windows 95 application. The 16-bit version also works on Windows 3.x; the 32-bit version tested with Windows NT 4.0.

Contact Zugg Software, Inc., at www.zuggsoft.com for more information.

IRC & Online Chat Index

10 Commandments of Online Chat 205–207

A

America Online (AOL) 25–64, 172–177
    Abbreviations (or acronyms) 30–31
    Emoticons 31–32
    Guides 173
    Installing 25–30
    Instant Messages (IMs) 36
    IRC 37–48
    Kids Only (KO) hosts 174–175
    Online help 172–177
    Passwords 29–30
    People Connection Hosts 173–174
    Rangers 173
    Screen name 27–29
    Virtual Places 52–55
Attention seekers 101–109

B

Bits 18
Buffer 18–19
Bytes 18

C

Carding 186–187
Chatting
    See also **Online chat** *or* **Online rules**
    10 Commandments of Online Chat 205–207

America Online 25–64
Electronic bulletin boards 49–52
Enhanced CUSeeMe 56–59
Proper behavior while chatting 79–96
Rules to follow when chatting 67–75
Shorthands 30–36
Tips on chatting 67–75, 80–96
Types of people chatting 132–136
Videophone 60–62
Ways to chat poorly 88–95
Web-based chats 49
Web-based conference chats 55–56
Why people chat 132–166
Chatting (what to avoid) . 88–95, 161–164, 177–198
    Carding 186–187
    Character role 90–92
    Cracking 188–189
    Cyberpunks 190–191
    Flaming 92–95
    Online stalkers 195–198
    Personal attacks 92–95
    Phishers 180–186
    Phreakers 192–193
    Phreaking 162
    Pornography 162–164
    Snert 88–90
    Wannabes 195
    Warez 187–189
    Warez rooms 161–162
    Whacker 193–194
    Wormers 189–190

Index

Chatting (Why people chat) 132–166
   Areas to avoid 161–164
   Curiosity 158–161
   Games 138–141
   Meet people 136–137
   MUD (Multi-User Dungeon) 141–155
   Resources 158–161
   Romance 164–165
   Safe forums 155–157
   Support 165–167
   Who is chatting 132–136
Chatting safety 171–202
   "Bad guys" 177–198
   Carding 186–187
   Cracking 188–189
   Cyberpunks 190–191
   "Good guys" 172–177
   Meeting people offline 200–202
   Online help 172–177
   Online stalkers 195–198
   Passwords 198–200
   Phishers 180–186
   Phreakers 192–193
   Security measures 198–202
   Wannabes 195
   Warez 187–189
   Whacker 193–194
   Wormers 189–190
Chatting tips 80–88
   Be conversational 85–87
   Be yourself 81
   Keep your own personality 87–88
   Participate 81–83
   Type the way you speak 84–85
   Ways to chat poorly 88–95
Communication protocol 15
   IP 15
   TCP 15
Companion CD-ROM 3–5, 218–234
   Active Worlds 221–222
   AtChat 219–220
   Contents 4–5, 218–234
   CU-See Me 222–223
   ichat 225
   Installing 3–5

   IRCFerret & WebFerret 223–224
   LOL Chat 225–227
   Masquerade 227–228
   mIRC 228–229
   NetGammon 229
   Pager 230–231
   PowWow 231
   PowWow for Kids! 232
   WhitePineBoard 232–233
   zMUD Connector 233–234
Cracking 188–189
CUSeeMe 211
Cyberpunks 190–191

D

Dealing with inappropriate behavior 116–128

E

Electronic bulletin boards 49–52
Emoticons 31–32, 211
Enhanced CUSeeMe 56–59

F

Firewall 212
Flame 212
Flaming 92
FOD 89

G

Glossary 210–215
   See also **Terminology**
GUI (Graphic User Interface) 15
Guides 173

H

Harassing people and online chat 70–71
Hard drive 17–18

236

Index

I

Impersonation and online chat 72–73
Impolite or forward suggestors 109–111
Inappropriate behavior 99–128
    Attention seekers 101–109
    Dealing with inappropriate behavior 116–128
    Impolite or forward suggestors 109–111
    Scrolling or flooding 102–108
    Spamming 111–116
    Types 100–116
    Types of inappropriate behavior 100–116
    Uppercase attention seekers 108
    WAV files attention seekers 108–109
Instant Messages (IMs) 36
Internet 25–64
Introduction to online chat 9–21
    Terminology 13–19
IP 15
IRC (Internet Relay Chat) 37–48, 212

K

Keyword TOS (for Terms of Service) 69
Kids Only (KO) hosts 174–175

L

Lurk 138
Lurker 81

M

Modem 14
MOO (MUD Object Oriented) 141
MOTD (Message of the Day) 69
MUD (Multi-User Dungeon) 141–155
    Choosing a MUD 152–155
    Commands 149–150
    Rules and suggestions 148–149
    Tips 151–152
    Using 142–155
MUSH (Multi-User Shared Hallucination) 141

N

Netiquette 27, 213

O

Online chat
    See also **Chatting**
    Dealing with inappropriate behavior 116–128
    Inappropriate behavior 99–128
    Introduction 9–21
    What to do 20–21
Online chats (what to avoid)
    Inappropriate behavior 99–128
Online help 172–177
Online rules 67–75
    Harassing people 70–71
    Impersonation 72–73
    Keyword TOS (for Terms of Service) 69
    MOTD (Message of the Day) 69
    Room disruption 73
    Scrolling 73
    Sexually explicit 72
    Unwritten rules of online chat 74
    Vulgarity 69–70
    Written rules 69–73
Online stalkers 195–198
Operating system 17

P

People Connection Hosts 173–174
Peripherals 14
Phishers 180–186
Phreakers 162, 192–193
Pornography 162–164
Processor (CPU) 14
Proper behavior while chatting 79–96
    Tips on chatting 80–88

R

RAM and ROM 16–17
Rangers 173
Room disruption and online chat 73

237

Index

S

Scrolling and online chat 73
Scrolling or flooding 102–108
Server 214
Sexually explicit and online chat 72
Shareware 215
Shorthands 30–36, 215
    Abbreviations (or acronyms) 30–31
    Emoticons 31–32
Snert 88
Spam and Spamming 101, 111–116, 215

T

TCP 15
Telnet 215
Telnet application 50–52
Terminology 13–19
    See also **Glossary**

U

Unwritten rules of online chat 74
Uppercase attention seekers 108

V

Video card 16
Videophone 60–62
Virtual Places 52–55
Vulgarity and online chat 69–70

W

Wannabes 195
Warez 161–162, 187–189
WAV files attention seekers 108–109
Web-based chats 49
Web-based conference chats 55–56
Whacker 193–194
Window 19
Wormers 189–190

238

PC catalog

Order Toll Free 1-800-451-4319
Books and Software

www.abacuspub.com

To order direct call Toll Free 1-800-451-4319

In US and Canada add $5.00 shipping and handling. Foreign orders add $13.00 per item.
Michigan residents add 6% sales tax.

Developers Series books are for professional software developers who require in-depth technical information and programming techniques.

PC Intern—6th Edition
The Encyclopedia of System Programming

Now in its 6th Edition, more than 500,000 programmers worldwide rely on the authoritative and eminently understandable information in this one-of-a-kind volume. You'll find hundreds of practical, working examples written in assembly language, C++, Pascal and Visual Basic—all professional programming techniques which you can use in your own programs. PC INTERN is a literal encyclopedia for the PC programmer. PC INTERN clearly describes the aspects of programming under all versions of DOS as well as interfacing with Windows.

Includes CD-ROM with Sample Programs

Some of the topics include:
- Memory organization on the PC
- Writing resident TSR programs
- Programming graphic and video cards
- Using extended and expanded memory
- Handling interrupts in different languages
- Networking programming NetBIOS and IPX/SPX
- Win95 virtual memory and common controls
- IRQs—programming interrupt controllers
- Understanding DOS structures and function
- Using protected mode, DOS extenders and DPMI/VCPI multiplexer
- Programming techniques for CD-ROM drives
- Programming Sound Blaster and compatibles

The companion CD-ROM transforms PC INTERN from a book into an interactive reference. You can search, navigate and view the entire text of the book and have instant access to information using hypertext links. Also included on the CD-ROM are hundreds of pages of additional programming tables and hard-to-find material.

Author: Michael Tischer and Bruno Jennrich
Order Item: #B304
ISBN: 1-55755-304-1

SRP: $69.95 US/$99.95 CAN
with companion CD-ROM

To order direct call Toll Free 1-800-451-4319

In US and Canada add $5.00 shipping and handling. Foreign orders add $13.00 per item. Michigan residents add 6% sales tax.

Productivity Series books are for users who want to become more productive with their PC.

Upgrading and Maintaining Your PC
New Sixth Edition!

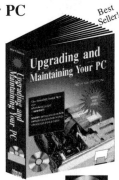

Buying a personal computer is a major investment. Today's fast-changing technology and innovations, such as Windows NT, ISDN cards and super fast components, require that you upgrade to keep your system current. New hardware and software developments require more speed, more memory and larger capacities. This book is for the millions of PC owners who want to retain their sizable investment in their PC system by upgrading.

With current info on the newest technology, *Upgrading & Maintaining Your PC* starts by helping readers make informed purchasing decisions. Whether it's a larger hard drive, more memory or a new CD-ROM drive, you'll be able to buy components with confidence.

CD-ROM INCLUDED!

Inside this new 6th Edition:
- Over 200 Photos and Illustrations
- Upgrader's guide to shopping for PC motherboards, operating systems, I/O cards, processors and more!
- Windows NT Workstation 4.0, Windows 95 and OS/2 Warp 4.0
- Processors(Intel, Cyrix, AMD and more), Internal/External cache
- The latest video and sound cards and installation tips
- **SPECIAL WINDOWS 95 SECTION!**

On the CD-ROM-
•**Wintune**—Windows Magazine's system tune-up program • **SYSINFO**—system"quick glance" program • **Cyrix Test**—Cyrix upgrade processor test • **P90 TEST**—the famous Intel Pentium "math" test • **WinSleuth**—Windows diagnostic utility • **And Much More!**

Publisher: Abacus
Order Item #S325
ISBN: 1-55755-329-7

Suggested Retail Price
$44.95 US/$59.95 CAN
CD-ROM Software Included

To order direct call Toll Free 1-800-451-4319

In US & Canada Add $5.00 Shipping and Handling
Foreign Orders Add $13.00 per item. Michigan residents add 6% sales tax.

Productivity Series books are for users who want to become more productive with their PC.

Your Family Tree
Using Your PC

Your Family Tree is a beginners guide to researching, organizing and sharing your family's heritage with relatives and friends. If you want to trace your family roots, get started by using this book and companion CD-ROM.

Author Jim Oldfield, Jr. shows how to get started tracing your roots using his expert, easy-to-follow steps and your personal computer. An experienced genealogist, Jim has produced three family history books of his own, and now you can too.

You'll learn how to gather facts and information, transfer them to popular genealogy programs, add illustrations, use your word processor or desktop publisher to produce reports, share the info in a meaningful way and keep up with 'newer' family additions.

Topics discussed include:
- Researching on the Internet
- Creating a Web site for your family pages
- Starting your own newsletter or association
- Adding photos and sound to your family tree
- Using conversion programs to publish data on the Web
- Using software like- Family Tree, Family Origins and more

CD-ROM INCLUDED!

On the CD-ROM-

The companion CD-ROM has various family pedigree forms for collecting family information, sample family data that shows you 'hands-on' how to get started, family photos and a collection of the most popular shareware for genealogy and illustrations.

Author: Jim Oldfield, Jr.
Order Item #B310
ISBN: 1-55755-310-6

Suggested Retail Price
$25.95 US/$34.95 CAN
CD-ROM Included

To order direct call Toll Free 1-800-451-4319

In US & Canada Add $5.00 Shipping and Handling
Foreign Orders Add $13.00 per item. Michigan residents add 6% sales tax.

Beginner's Series
easy learning for everyone

CD-ROM Included

Paint Shop Pro for Beginners
"no experience required"

Paint Shop Pro is an award-winning graphics application and one of the most popular shareware products in the world. This beginner's book takes a first-time users approach to learning and working with Paint Shop Pro 3.12 for Windows 95 and Windows 3.X. you'll discover what plug-ins and filters are, how to create special effects and then onto working with your very first image.

Author Scott Slaughter takes a "how-to" approach to the book and illustrates the steps involved in doing things like fixing a treasured photo, adding color, converting images to any of the 30 different formats available and why. Paint Shop Pro is an ideal utility for creating the kind of GIF files required of the Internet. In addition you'll learn how to perform screen captures and numerous tips & tricks used by the pros.

Other topics include:

- Working with image files
- Zooming, cropping, and moving images
- Paint tool techniques like airbrushing and flood fill
- Learn to use select tools such as the clone brush, lasso, and magic wand
- Working with color palettes
- Deformations and special effects
- Retouching photos

The companion CD-ROM includes a fully-functional evaluation version of Paint Shop Pro 3.12 for Windows 95 and Windows 3.X.

Author: Scott Slaughter
Item #: B319
ISBN: 1-55755-319-X
SRP: $19.95 US/26.95 CAN
  with CD-ROM

Order Direct Toll Free 1-800-451-4319

In US and Canada add $5.00 shipping and handling. Foreign orders add $13.00 per item.
Michigan residents add 6% sales tax.

Beginners Series books are for users who want to become more productive with their PC's.

Easy Digital Photography

Easy Digital Photography will introduce you to the growing field of digital photography. It takes a first-time users approach to working with digital cameras, scanners and image editors. Includes useful descriptions of how digital cameras and scanners work and information on what to look for when buying a digital camera or a scanner.

You'll also learn about image editors and how to use an image editor to "tweak" your photos.

Easy Digital Photography shows how to use the mix of popular name brand hardware and software that is quickly changing the face of photography. It's a "how-to" guide that teaches how to make photography for the PC easy, practical, affordable, and fun!

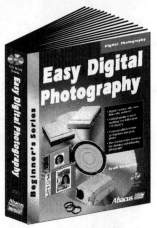

You'll learn to do more with your photos than you ever could before.

Topics discussed include:
- Step-by-step tips on using image editors, digital cameras and scanners
- Overcoming common problems
- New FlashPix technology
- Video capture devices
- Digital images and the Internet

CD-ROM INCLUDED!

On the CD-ROM:

The companion CD-ROM includes evaluation and demonstration versions of popular commercial software, such as PhotoStudio from Arcsoft and PhotoSuite from MGI. It also includes a wealth of sample images and selected image conversion programs.

Author: Scott Slaughter
Order Item #B330
ISBN: 1-55755-330-0

Suggested Retail Price
$29.95 US/$39.95 CAN
CD-ROM Included

To order direct call Toll Free 1-800-451-4319

In US & Canada Add $5.00 Shipping and Handling
Foreign Orders Add $13.00 per item. Michigan residents add 6% sales tax.

Visit our website at www.abacuspub.com

Don't Forget To Visit Our Web Site

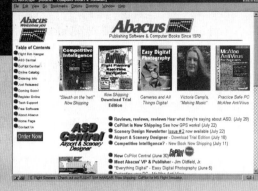

Now you can find all the latest information about Abacus and Abacus products at our web site: **http://www.abacuspub.com**.

The Web site includes an online catalog so you can find out what you need to know about a title. You can also preview upcoming books and software. Have a question you need answered? Send Email to our technicians, customer service reps and editors right from our web site.

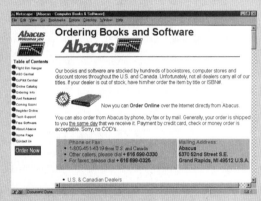

The web site shows how you can order Abacus products; you can even order online over the Internet directly from Abacus.

If you have a question or a problem with one of our books or software titles, we may already have the answer for you. Our FAQs are arranged under "Books" and "Software" icons. Simply click the desired icon to see the information.

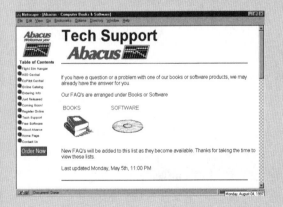

www.abacuspub.com

What You'll Find On The Companion CD-ROM

Welcome to the IRC & Online Chat companion CD-ROM. We hope this book will be an indispensable reference guide to the world of IRC and online chat. The companion CD-ROM includes the best chat software for you to evaluate. See Chapter 1 for information on installing and using the companion CD-ROM. Also, see Appendix B for complete information on the contents of the companion CD-ROM.

What are the chat software titles that you'll find on the companion CD-ROM. Well, they include the following:

See Chapter 1 and Appendix B for more information about the companion CD-ROM

- ❖ AtChat from Abbott Systems Inc.
- ❖ Active Worlds by Worlds, Inc.
- ❖ CU-See Me from White Pines Software, Inc.
- ❖ IRCFerret & WebFerret from FerretSoft LLC
- ❖ ichat by ichat, inc.
- ❖ LOL Chat from LOL Software, Inc.
- ❖ Masquerade from HiJiNX Interactive Entertainment
- ❖ mIRC from mIRC Co., LTD
- ❖ NetGammon from GOTO
- ❖ Pager from ichat, Inc.
- ❖ PowWow from Tribal Voice
- ❖ PowWow for KIDS! from Tribal Voice
- ❖ WhitePineBoard from White Pine Software, Inc.
- ❖ The zMUD Connector (Zugg's Multi-User Dungeon) by Andrew Cowan